WITHDRAWN

Common Learning

Common Learning

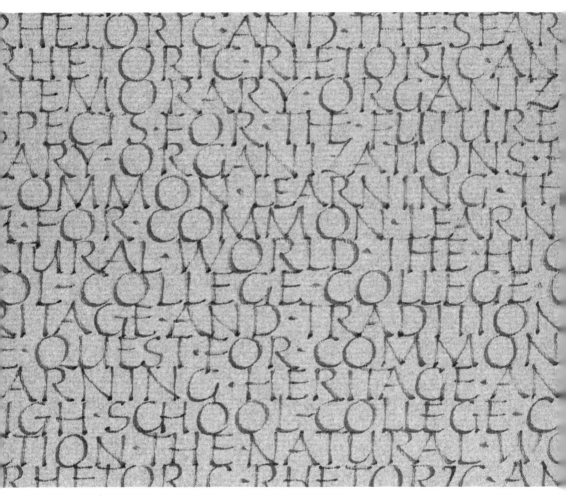

THE CARNEGIE FOUNDATION
FOR THE ADVANCEMENT OF TEACHING

A Carnegie Colloquium on General Education

1785 Massachusetts Avenue, N.W.,
Washington, D.C. 20036

The Carnegie Foundation for the Advancement of Teaching

Designed by Julian Waters, Bookmark Studio

Manufactured in the United States of America

Contents

Preface

*J*f not a revival, then something very much like it is happening in general education in the 1980s. Visiting colleges and universities across the country one learns that the subject is a major topic of discussion in formal conferences and committee meetings, in seminars, and over luncheon in faculty clubs. The revival has missionaries among men and women who teach in nearly all of the academic disciplines. And it has aroused the interest of administrators, faculty members, and students alike.

Evidence of this revival was presented earlier this year in an essay entitled *A Quest for Common Learning.* In that essay, Arthur Levine, Senior Fellow of our Foundation, and I defined general education as "the learning that should be common to all people." Summarized in chapters one and seven of this volume, the essay reviews the current status of general education, which we consider to be in shambles; surveys the history of recent general education revivals; provides a rationale for general education; employs that rationale to evaluate current practices; and offers proposals for future action.

Our essay on common learning provided the theme for a national Colloquium on Common Learning held at the University of Chicago in April, 1981, with the sponsorship of The Carnegie Foundation of Teaching and the Charles A. Dana Foundation. About 200 participants, including college and university presidents, academic deans, faculty members, and students heard distinguished speakers address the general education theme from different disciplinary perspectives. Those addresses have been adapted as chapters in *Common Learning.*

The Colloquium on Common Learning was in many ways a "town meeting" of educators. Participants not only listened to the featured speakers, they responded — asking questions, reporting general education proposals on their own campuses, providing practical suggestions. Regrettably, there is no way to capture, in this book, the interest and enthusiasm of the participants. WGBH Education Foundation in Boston recorded the event, however, and edited the proceedings for presentation as a brief program on videocassettes that are available from our Foundation.

Neither the original essay, *A Quest for Common Learning*, the videocassettes, nor this book provide ultimate answers to questions about what a general education program ought to be. Those answers will be different for every school or college. We do hope, however, that these efforts will raise the level of the general education debate, and focus attention less on the politics of general education and more on its substance.

On behalf of The Carnegie Foundation for the Advancement of Teaching, I want to thank those who contributed so significantly to the Foundation's general education program. In particular, I am most grateful to the contributors to this volume. As participants in our colloquium and authors of the chapters on the following pages, these distinguished scholars have set a high standard for discourse on common learning. We also appreciate the generosity of The Charles A. Dana Foundation, which made the colloquium possible, and extend special thanks to President Hannah H. Gray, and her staff at the University of Chicago, for the gracious hospitality extended to all of those who participated in it.

ERNEST L. BOYER
President
The Carnegie Foundation for the
Advancement of Teaching
July, 1981

Common Learning

The Quest
for Common Learning

BY ERNEST L. BOYER

CHAPTER ONE

*A*ny serious study of general education must ultimately, if not initially, confront a very basic question: What education should be common to all people? Arthur Levine and I came to that conclusion very early in our own study of general education. After looking at hundreds of catalogs and visiting dozens of colleges and universities, we concluded that general education on most campuses is in disarray. On many campuses, in fact, it has become the spare room of academic life, and, like all spare rooms, it is chronically in a state ranging from casual neglect to serious disrepair. In the absence of clearcut goals, a hodge-podge of uses and misuses has been spawned, and a plethora of incoherent programs has emerged. At too many campuses, we found evidence that very few faculty members held any convictions about what all students need to know.

On a more hopeful note, however, we saw that something else is in the wind. There is a growing swell of concern for general education all across the country. Most of the institutions we visited are revising their curricula in one way or another, and the current flurry of activity appears to be nothing less than a national revival.

Since the turn of the century, we have had two other times when enthusiasm for reform swept across our nation's campuses.

The first such revival occurred at about the time of World War I. In 1914, President Alexander Meiklejohn of Amherst College introduced a survey course entitled "Social and Economic Institutions." Five years later, Columbia University launched a similar course called "Contemporary Civilization" which was required for all freshmen. Dartmouth and Reed followed suit with survey courses of their own. But, the most hotly debated experiment of this period was "The College" at the University of Chicago. It was a radical approach embodying, among other things, great books, comprehensive examinations, and a four-year, fully required course of study. The prestige of the university, and the charisma of Robert Hutchins caught the nation's fancy.

This general education revival was very much a reflection of the times. Teddy Roosevelt's "Square Deal" and Woodrow Wilson's "New Freedom" crusade had ended. The so-called Progressive Era — with its concern for municipal reform, corporate regulation, and welfare legislation — faded.

As the social historian Frederick Lewis Allen put it, the nation in the 1920s was "spiritually tired":

Wearied by the excitements of the war and the nervous tension of the big Red Scare (1919-20) [Americans] hoped for quiet and healing. There might be no such word in the dictionary as normalcy, but normalcy was what they wanted. [1]

In the midst of this drift toward personal and national isolation, general education was revived. For some, a core of common learning provided a weapon against the misplaced vocational emphasis of the 1920s. Others believed that colleges and universities had gone too far in catering to individual interests. But, above all, for older Americans still rooted in the pre-War certitudes, general education would combat the cynicism and disillusionment of the younger generation. It would revive, as well, the sense of national unity that had so suddenly and so mysteriously faded with the signing of the Armistice.

Interestingly, while this general education revival was sparked by events beyond the campus, its decline was hastened by another noncampus crisis, the Great Depression. Students, like all other Americans, wanted jobs, and decreasing college attendance rates halted the revival.

The second general education movement of this century came on the heels of World War II. Franklin D. Roosevelt's "New Deal" was overshadowed by world holocaust, and once again, Americans turned inward.

Joseph C. Goulden, in *The Best Years*, his popularized account of the years following World War II, said the United States:

...went into a holding period intellectually, morally, politically.... The result was a generation content to put its trust in government and in authority, to avoid deviant political ideas, to enjoy material comfort without undue worry about the invisible, intrinsic costs. America misplaced, somewhere and somehow, the driving moral force it carried out of the world war.... There were times, during the 1950s, when the entire nation seemed to be saying, "Leave me alone."[2]

During this quiescent period, the nation's preoccupation was more personal and less social. Altruism declined. Charitable contributions fell off, yet expenditures on personal items, such as jewelry and clothing, increased. After the shortages of the depression and the fatigue of the war, a "catch up" mentality spread across the land.

But on the nation's campuses, a more reflective, more sober attitude was stirring. World War II had been a profound intellectual and spiritual shock to many academics. Germany, that great center of scholarship, had spawned monstrous inhumanity, and Buchenwald and Auschwitz seemed to mock decades of lofty rhetoric about education's ennobling and civilizing power.

It was against this somber background that American education began to ponder, once again, the place of general education in academic life. In 1942, Denison University offered a core course entitled "Problems of Peace and Post-War Reconstruction." Later, Wesleyan University, in Connecticut, introduced a freshman general education seminar. But it was the 1945 Harvard report on *General Education in a Free Society*, the "Redbook,"[3] that was the nation's symbol of renewal. It became the Bible on campuses from coast to coast, even though in Cambridge itself the Harvard faculty rejected its proposals.

As in the 1930s, it was another dramatic national crisis, this time *Sputnik*, that dampened the revival. The Soviet satellite shocked the nation, and a wave of specialization with emphasis on science, foreign languages, and programs for the gifted swept the campuses.

General education was further battered by the turbulence of the 1960s, when it was attacked by radicals and reformers alike for its rigidity, its narrowness, and its failure to meet the need of traditionally bypassed students.

"Relevance" and "diversity" became the new shibboleths to be worshipped.

*T*o a remarkable degree, the earlier general education revivals of this century were products of times when war destroyed community, when political participation declined, when government efforts to set a common social agenda weakened, when international isolationism was on the rise, and when individual altruism decreased.

From 1914 to the present, general education spokesmen worried about a society that appeared to be losing cohesion, splintering into countless individual atoms, each flying off in its own direction, each pursuing its own selfish ends. Each general education revival, therefore, moved in the direction of community and away from social fragmentation. The focus, consistently, was on shared values, shared responsibilities, shared governance, a shared heritage, and a shared world vision. This is an important point, because it suggests that the ebb and flow of general education is, in fact, a mirror of broader shifts in the nation's mood.

General education advocates have also been convinced that our common life must be reaffirmed, our common goals redefined, our common problems confronted. The specific agenda varied, but the underlying concern has remained remarkably constant. It reflects the never-ending tension between the individual and the group, between freedom and control, between independence and interdependence.

All societies, John Locke argued, are bound together by a social contract, a compact among individuals who cede a portion of their autonomy for the greater good. In most societies, the terms of the contract seem to move first in one direction, then another. When too great an emphasis is placed on group relationship, individuals feel herded, smothered, and restrained. In contrast, when the pendulum swings strongly toward independence, people are apt to feel alone, isolated in an apathetic and uncaring world.

This perennial tension between our aloneness and our oneness is mirrored, we believe, in the college curriculum. The elective portion of the curriculum acknowledges the right of each person to act independently and make personal choices. So does an academic major. General education is a different matter. This portion of the curriculum is rooted in the belief that individualism, while essential, is not sufficient. It says that individuals also share significant relationships with a larger community.

Through general education on the one hand, and majors and electives on the other, the college curriculum recognizes both our independence *and* our interdependence. It acknowledges the necessary balance between individual preferences and community needs. Just as we search politically and socially to maintain the necessary balance between the two, so, in education, we seek the same end.

This is not to say that general education should promote intellectual conformity. We are not talking about a spurious "togetherness" or an artificial consensus where none, in fact, exists. Quite the opposite. The kind of general education we envisage will focus on issues about which people feel most deeply, on points where conflict and controversy are most likely to occur. What will be shared is not a common set of conclusions, but a common agenda.

What then, do we see as the agenda for general education? Simply stated, it is those experiences, relationships, and ethical concerns that are common to all of us simply by virtue of our membership in the human family at a particular moment in history. General education is an institutional affirmation of society's claim on its members.

This description of general education is not particularly novel. Woodrow Wilson, when he was president of Princeton, called for a general education that would focus on the common experiences, the common thoughts and struggles, the old triumphs and defeats. And Mark Van Doren of Columbia University once spoke of "the connectedness of things"[4] as a major concern of educators.

This emphasis on our "connectedness" should, however, be reaffirmed, not as a nostalgic return to a neglected tradition, but because it is urgently required. Today's students are the products of a society in which the call for individual gratification booms forth on every side while the social claim is weak and enfeebled. Today's freshmen were one year old when John Kennedy was killed. They were six when Johnson's Great Society ended, when Robert Kennedy and Martin Luther King were assassinated, and when our cities were burned in riots. They were eleven when the United States disengaged from Vietnam. And they were twelve when the President of the United States resigned from office in disgrace while other high administration officials were imprisoned as criminals. When undergraduates were asked which events most influenced their thinking, they answered most frequently "Watergate" and "Vietnam."

Today's young people are understandably more cynical and less optimistic than their recent predecessors. They are educationally more competitive, more geared toward training for jobs, and more committed to getting higher grades. Although students are optimistic about their own futures, believing they will get good jobs, good money, and good things, they are pessimistic about the future of the nation and the world. They are more committed to their personal futures than to the future we face together.

Sadly, most colleges exacerbate this tendency toward self-preoccupation and social isolation. The academic major and electives, with their emphasis on individual interests, are made the centerpiece of collegiate study, while general education is in shambles. On campus after campus, there is no agreement about the meaning of a college education. We are more confident about the length of the baccalaureate degree program than we are about its substance.

Simply stated, the mission of general education is to help students understand that they are not only autonomous individuals, but also members of a human community to which they are accountable. In education, as in life itself, one aspect of our being must not eclipse the other. In calling for a reaffirmation of general education, our aim is to help restore the balance. Rather than continuing to be the spare room in the house of intellect, general education must have a central purpose of its own.

At a recent meeting of the American Association for the Advancement of Science, Dr. Lewis Thomas, acknowledging that these are not the best of times for the human mind, went on to observe:

I cannot begin to guess at all the causes of our cultural sadness, not even the most important ones, but I can think of one thing that is wrong with us and eats away at us: we do not know enough about how we work, about where we fit in, and most of all about the enormous, imponderable system of life in which we are embedded as working parts.[5]

Dr. Thomas concluded by saying "if this century does not slip forever through our fingers, it will be because learning will have directed us away from our splintered dumbness and will have helped us focus on our common goals."

This sums up both purpose and the urgency of general education.

But what are those areas of interdependence that should be studied by all students? Obviously, many different lists could be drawn up.

For purposes of discussion, we have identified six connections, six broad themes, that we believe to be the proper concern of general education. An exploration of these connections is indispensable if students are adequately to understand themselves, their society, and the world in which they live.

First, all students should come to understand the shared use of symbols.

The sending and receiving of messages separates human beings from all other forms of life. Language is the connecting tissue that binds society together, and we propose that all students, from the very first years of formal schooling, learn not only to "read and write," but also to read with understanding, write with clarity, and listen and speak effectively.

In addition, all students should become proficient in the use of numbers, which constitute an essential and universally accepted symbol system, too. The master of these skills is the foundation of common learning. Without them, the goals of general education will be fatally undermined.

But developing language skills, as important as this may be, is not enough. Students should also come to understand why and how language has evolved, how messages reveal the values of a culture, how words and thoughts interact, and how feelings and ideas are conveyed through literature.

The study of a *second* language is particularly important, not just because of its direct utility but also because such a study helps students view language freshly and see how language reflects cultural values and traditions.

Students should explore, as well, how we communicate nonverbally, through music, dance, and the visual arts. They should understand how these forms of expression convey subtle meanings, express intense emotions, and how, uniquely, the arts can stir a deep response in others.

The impact of mass communication should also be examined. In the United States, children watch television 6,000 hours before they spend a single hour in the classroom. Students urgently need what might be called "tube literacy," to help them see how visual and auditory signals reinforce each other, how ideas can be distorted, and how thoughts and feelings can be subliminally conveyed.

We are convinced that in the days ahead, the language of computers merits study, too. Every generally educated student should learn about this pervasive signal system that increasingly controls our day-to-day transactions.

The goals we have just proposed are ambitious. But, they are essential if students are to survive in a world where symbols give individuals their identities, where message-sending makes transactions possible, and where language provides the foundation for all further learning.

Second, all students should understand their shared membership in groups and institutions.

We are born into institutions, we pass much of our lives in institutions, and institutions are involved when we die. The general education curriculum we have in mind would look at the origin of institutions; how they evolve, grow strong, become oppressive or weak, and sometimes disappear.

In addition to this broad-gauge approach, we suggest a more inductive study, one that looks more penetratingly at a *single* institution—the Peace Corps; the Teamsters Union; the city council; or one related, perhaps, to a student's special field of interest. How did the institution begin? What were its initial purposes? What new missions has it assumed? To whom is it accountable? Is the institution still vital, or is it being maintained only because of ceremony and tradition?

The goal should be to help students see that everyone shares membership in the "common institutions" of our culture — those social structures that shape our lives, impose obligations, restrict choices, and provide services that we could not obtain in isolation.

Third, students should understand that everyone produces and consumes and that, through this process, we are dependent on each other.

Specifically, we propose that students explore the significance of work in the lives of individuals and examine how work patterns reflect the values and shape the social climate of a culture. Such a curriculum would ask: What have been the historical, philosophical, religious, and social attitudes toward work around the world? How are notions about work related to social status and human dignity? What determines the different status and rewards we grant to different forms of work? Why is some work highly rewarded and other work relatively unrewarded? In addition, general education should help students discover that work, at its very best, can be life-fulfilling.

We do not suggest that the nation's colleges and universities become vocational institutions. But producing and consuming are central to our common experience. They are the ways we define ourselves. Their study, we believe, can be a legitimate, demanding part of general education.

Fourth, all life forms on the planet earth are inextricably interlocked, and no education is complete without an understanding of the ordered, interdependent nature of the universe.

General education means learning about the elegant, underlying patterns of the natural world and discovering that all elements of nature are, in some manner, related to each other.

K. Danner Clouser, "Philosopher-in-Residence" at Pennsylvania State University College of Medicine, says that most students, even after an introductory course in biology or chemistry "have little grasp of how it (science) works, of what its genius consists, what its theories are, how they are tested and what defeats them . . . Science is, for them, a catalog of facts . . . complete and beyond question."[6]

We believe students should be introduced not just to the "facts" of science, but also to its processes. They should understand how science is a process of trial and error; how, through observation and testing, theories are found, refined, sometimes discarded, and often give rise to other theories. Students should learn about the applications of science and see how scientific discoveries have led to a flood of inventions and new technologies that have brought with them both benefits and risks.

Finally, there is the matter of science and citizenship. The British novelist and scientist C. P. Snow said that between science and society there lies "a gulf of mutual incomprehension."[7] Unfortunately, this gulf is widening at the very time policy issues of great significance must be urgently examined. If students are intelligently to evaluate the pros and cons of nuclear power, space exploration, food additives, and pollution standards, they must become more knowledgeable about underlying facts and principles behind the headlines.

Becoming a responsible human being in the last quarter of

the twentieth century means learning about the great power of science, its pervasive influence in all aspects of our life, and our own shared relationship with nature.

This is an essential part of common learning.

Fifth, all students should understand our shared sense of time.

Our common heritage is a bridge that holds us all together in ways we hardly understand. It is more than this. It is what Edmund Burke termed "a pact between the dead, the living, and the yet unborn." It is essential that the human race remember where it has been and how, for better or worse, it got where it is. An understanding of our shared heritage should be expected of all students.

We propose a study that focuses on the seminal ideas and events that have decisively shaped the course of history. More than a collection of facts, this approach would emphasize the convergence of social, religious, political, economic, and intellectual forces. In such a study no attempt should be made to worship coverage. Choices must be made. To select a few themes carefully and explore them intensively across disciplinary lines is entirely appropriate, we believe, to the goals of common learning.

One further point. All human beings look in *two* directions. We recall the past and anticipate the future. Both perspectives determine, at least in part, how we behave today. "What do we predict for the 1980s?" or "What will life be like in the year 2000?" could only be asked by those with a sense of a shared tomorrow. Indeed the labels "past" and "future" are, in a fundamental sense, distinctions without meaning. T. S. Eliot wrote: "Time present and time past are both present in time future, and time future contained in time past. . . ."[8]

Most scholars are understandably reluctant to speculate

about a world that is yet to be. They are unwilling to be identified, even obliquely, with professional "futurologists" who predict progress or disaster with equal certainty. Despite this reluctance, general education should, we believe, help all students understand how past visions of the future have shaped the course of history. Exploring our shared sense of time is, we believe, a central part of common learning.

Finally, all students should explore our shared values and beliefs.

Inherent in our relationships with others are patterns of agreed-upon behaviors — laws, customs, and traditions that reflect widely shared beliefs. In traveling around the world, one is struck more by the similarities than by the differences of people, more by the predictability than by the unpredictability of human behavior.

All individuals and societies are continuously making choices, revising their standards of conduct, debating "right" and "wrong," deciding what currently is good and what is best.

A study of the personal and social significance of shared values should be the capstone to common learning. Each student should identify the premises inherent in his or her own beliefs, learn how to make responsible decisions, and discuss the ethical and moral choices that confront us all.

Such a study relates directly to the general education themes we have just discussed. In every one of these shared experiences, moral and ethical choices must be made. How, for example, can messages be honestly and effectively conveyed? How can institutions serve the needs of both the individual *and* the group? On what basis is a vocation selected or rejected? Where can the line be drawn between conservation and exploitation of natural resources? These are only a few of the consequential ethical and moral issues that a common learning curriculum must confront.

In the last analysis, we are persuaded by Bertrand Russell who said that "Without civic morality communities perish, without personal morality their survival has no value."[9] We do not suggest, of course, that colleges and universities should seek to impose a single set of values. Rather, the aim of general education should be to help students think clearly about how values are shaped, and how each one of us must build, and periodically review, an authentic, satisfying value structure of our own.

*I*n the end, each college and university faculty must shape a general education program to reflect its own unique values and traditions. The six general education themes we have described should be viewed as illustrations rather than a blueprint. Our purpose has been to initiate general education planning, not complete it.

The general education goals we have discussed cannot be achieved fully in any two-year sequence, or even a lifetime. At the same time, we believe that with careful planning, a good beginning can be made. For one thing, the first-year college student has already completed twelve years of formal education and the nation's colleges and universities should build on this foundation. The time has come for school and college leaders to work together to clarify the goals of common learning, and, as this partnership is forged, we are confident that the goals we have discussed can be more effectively achieved.

We wish to underscore another point. General education does not necessarily require the designing of new courses.

Existing departmental courses in English, history, sociology, or science may effectively fill the bill. But here we add a word of caution. It would be a great mistake to slip existing courses unexamined into a general education curriculum. The title of a course may sound appropriate to general education, and the catalogue description may be appealing. But the way the course is actually taught may, in fact, promote specialized, not general education.

When we force general education into discrete departmental containers, its purposes are frequently subverted. The focus is too narrow. Connections are not made.

When students are required to take a language course, a science course, and a history course, frequently they are simply introduced to these specialties from the point of view of a linguist, a scientist, and an historian. Each course has distinct boundaries; each inquiry is isolated from the other. Little thought is given to how the separate disciplines might actually contribute to a truly *general* education. If anything, the question is often posed the other way: how can general education contribute to the disciplines?

We are not suggesting that existing academic structures be abandoned. They are essential if scholarship is to be pursued. But we must also remember that the units of scholarly activity we call the disciplines have been organized for the purposes of specialization, not general education. They can be valuable allies of common learning, but they should not be viewed as its end.

*O*ne final note: We know that the barriers to general education are formidable. Departmental turf is jealously protected. Faculty members who devote themselves to general education run the risk of losing touch with their disciplines, and frequently they are not rewarded for their effort at tenure and promotion time.

Yet, without being unduly optimistic, we believe significant changes are in the wind. The contours of the disciplines are changing. New academic alliances are being formed. Interconnections between historically separate fields of study are emerging as inquiry on the frontiers of knowledge blend what traditionally have been isolated fields of study. Sociologists, psychologists, biologists, and chemists find themselves seeking answers to the same, or closely related questions. Humanists adopt some of the methods of the scientists while natural scientists ponder issues humanists have reflected upon for centuries.

Anthropologist Clifford Geertz of the Institute for Advanced Study at Princeton has gone so far as to describe these shifts in the world of scholarship as "an important change in the way we *think* about the way we think" [Emphasis ours]. This is reflected, Geertz says ". . . in philosophical inquiries that look like literary criticism (think of Stanley Cavell on Beckett or Thoreau, Sartre on Flaubert), scientific discussions that look like *belles lettres morceaux* (Lewis Thomas, Loren Eisley), baroque fantasies presented as straight forward empirical observations (Borges' Barthelme), or histories that consist of equations and tables or law court testimony (Fogel and Engerman, Le Roi Ladurie), documentaries that read like true confessions (Mailler), parables posing as ethnographies (Castenda), theoretical treatises set out as travelogues (Levi-Strauss), ideological arguments cast as historiographical inquiries (Edward Said), epistemological studies constructed like political tracts (Paul Feyerabend), methodological polemics got up as personal memoirs (James Watson)."[10]

Here is the point. The wall dividing the two cultures — scientific and humane—is still standing, but it is being continuously breached; the pattern of intellectual investigation is being rearranged. More than at any time in our memory, researchers feel the need to communicate with colleagues in other fields. And this epistemological change may have profound impact on the future of general education. As new investigative links are drawn, scholars at all levels will, of necessity, make new connections between their own disciplines and the disciplines of others. This more integrated view of knowledge and a focus on the larger questions in our teaching and research, will create, we believe, a climate favorable to general education in the nation's colleges and schools.

Nearly 40 years ago in *Liberal Education*, Mark Van Doren wrote:

The connectedness of things is what the educator contemplates to the limit of his capacity. No human capacity is great enough to permit a vision of the world as simple, but if the educator does not aim at the vision no one else will, and the consequences are dire when no one does. ... The student who can begin early in life to think of things as connected, even if he revises his view with every succeeding year, has begun the life of learning. [11]

Seeing "the connectedness of things," is, we conclude, the goal of common learning.

NOTES

1. Allen, Frederick L. *Only Yesterday: An Informal History of the 1920's* (New York, Harper and Row, 1964) pp. 103-104.

2. Goulden, Joseph C. *The Best Years: 1945-1950* (New York, Atheneum, 1976) pp. 427-428.

3. Harvard Committee. *General Education in a Free Society* (Cambridge, Harvard University Press, 1945).

4. Van Doren, Mark. *Liberal Education* (New York, Henry Holt, 1943) p. 115.

5. Thomas, Lewis. *The Medusa and the Snail: More Notes of a Biology Watcher* (New York, The Viking Press, 1979) p. 145.

6. Clouser, K. Danner. *The Role of the Humanities in Medical Education* (Norfolk, Teagle and Little, Inc., 1978) p. 28.

7. Snow, C. P. *The Two Cultures and the Scientific Revolution* (New York, Cambridge University Press, 1959) p. 4.

8. Eliot, T. S. "Burnt Norton" in *T. S. Eliot: The Complete Poems and Plays* (New York, Harcourt, Brace, and World, 1952) p. 117.

9. Russell, Bertrand. *Authority and the Individual* (New York, Simon and Shuster, 1949) p. 70

10. Geertz, Clifford. "Balanced Genres: The Refiguration of Social Thought," *American Scholar,* Spring 1980, vol. 49, no. 2, pp. 165-166.

11. Van Doren, Mark. *Liberal Education* (New York, Henry Holt, 1943) p. 115.

Mere Rhetoric, Rhetoric, & the Search for Common Learning

BY WAYNE C. BOOTH

CHAPTER TWO

*O*ne of my earliest experiences with curricular reform took place at Haverford College in the early fifties. After some months of careful thought about what was wrong with an absurd accretion of requirements that had never been thought through by anyone before, we on the Curriculum Committee had the instructive experience of seeing the faculty spend all of ten minutes on our report. The first blow was struck by someone's misquoting Samuel Johnson — something like: "Sir, debating a curriculum report is like debating about which leg of a boy's breeches should be put on first. You stand debating, first this leg and then that leg, and meanwhile the boy remains unbreeched." The coup de grace — only a pretentious cliché can do justice to it—the coup de grace was administered by kindly old Ned Snyder: "Gentlemen"—and we were all gentlemen in those days — "gentlemen, we are already the best men's college in the country. Why on earth we should change is more than I can see!"

The Haverford faculty, in its wisdom, assumed that it had debated the subject adequately, and dropped the report without a vote. The document disappeared without a trace.

I do not know that it was a good report; I never had a chance to find out by testing it in serious discussion—that is, in serious symbolic exchange in the search of shared convictions about education. What I know for sure is that our failure to debate its merits exhibited our bad rhetorical education, "highly educated" and well intentioned though we were. Skilled specialists, most of us, in the arts of reasoning in our specialties, we were totally unskilled — as many another faculty meeting at the time further revealed — in the art of reasoning together about shared concerns.

I must confess that having met our clones in many a meeting through almost thirty-five years of curricular discussion, I find our failure haunting us here as we renew deliberation about general education.

I may as well also confess that whenever I see a list of the essential ingredients of general education, I invariably feel that my own subjects have been radically underplayed. How could the Carnegie essayists be so blind as to list "The Shared Language and Symbols that Connect Us" as only one of six co-equal subjects, on a par with those other interesting but far less important subjects, history and natural science and ethics and political science? Have they not realized that the study of all the rest depends on the quality of the shared languages we use in that study? Have they not recognized that the study of how to improve our capacity to share symbols — what many of us call *rhetoric* — is thus the queen of the sciences?

I know very well that to succumb like that to the temptations of disciplinary imperialism is to destroy from the beginning any chance of our building a general education curriculum. So I feel guilty about such thoughts. But I would feel guiltier if I did not suspect that others secretly respond in the same way. The historians will wonder why history, which is obviously the most important and most neglected of studies, should be degraded to one-half of one slot out of six, and labelled only as a "concern with a common heritage,"—"as if we did not live and have our being in that heritage!" The natural scientists, the social scientists, and the philosophers similarly must each squirm a bit to see that what is for them central has been pinned wriggling to the wall-chart — and what is more, labelled with an alien name. And this is to say nothing about those other scholars and teachers who cannot find themselves on the chart at all. (You may have noticed how much we resemble, in our jockeyings for position in curricular debates, the various special interests in their responses to budget cutting proposals: insofar as we really care for our own territory, we almost inevitably place it ahead of all others.)

Such imperialisms aside, at least for the moment, I assume that we could all agree on something like the six-fold list in the Carnegie essay. We know that when our colleges graduate students who are radically ignorant and unskilled in these shared connections, the result is shocking. It is a scandal that so few of our graduates are even minimally proficient in more than one of the six fields. It is a scandal that even students who major in any one of the conventional fields that profess to deal with "connections" — I mention only English and philosophy — are often blind to the issues raised by words such as *shared* and *connections*. They have been systematically incapacitated for sharing anything except expertise with other experts in some subdivision of current inquiry. If you think I exaggerate, ask the next economics BA you meet what her study has taught her that would be useful in dealing with our rising mass illiteracy. Or try to have a good conversation about politics or literature with your university's MBAs or "behavioral psych" majors.

So far we might all agree, that sharing the six sharings will minimally mark a person as "generally educated," as someone we are not ashamed of. Presumably our next move is to discuss what particular consequences for educational planning might follow from such agreement. But experience teaches that trouble begins whenever we move from general goals to particular means.

Just think of the jealous responses we are likely to meet, within any one of the six general subjects — the sociologists, anthropologists, economists, legal theorists, and political scientists who will quarrel, for example, about which of them deals best with our "shared institutions" or "shared activities"; the various schools of philosophy, anthropology, psychology, and literary theory who will quarrel about which deals best with our "shared values"; and so on.

Or think of the academic rivals who might claim that they should provide the substance studied under the first category, "competence in symbol-sharing." Agreeing that students must become competent in "the shared language and symbols that connect us" — that they must learn to read, write, speak, and listen effectively — many different experts can make quite plausible cases for the centrality of what they do. Most obviously, teachers of composition and of elementary foreign languages will make their case for a basic literacy. But a basic literacy taught according to what paradigms? Offhand one can think of at least a dozen disciplines claiming to provide the central theory both for elementary instruction in how to read, think, speak, and write and for advanced training toward degrees: linguistics, semiotics, logic, analytical philosophy, hermeneutics, communications theory, various kinds of structuralism and deconstructionism — not to mention (as we say when mentioning) the many versions of my own pet field, rhetoric. And what about the fields that the report does mention but does not include explicitly in the summarizing chart — the languages of mathematics, of music, and of the visual arts? Where are the symbolic sharings through the languages of film, of photography, and of TV?

We all know that the same kinds of rivalry can be found under each of the other five categories, even in the natural sciences. What, then are we to do, when we turn from our general lists and try to design a general curriculum?

That question leads me nicely back to my own empire, rhetoric, just as it has led the Carnegie Foundation to place its money on the rhetoric of conferences and collections of essays in the hope of making changes in the world. Whenever we are faced with a multiplicity of seemingly conflicting spoken or written claims, what we all try to do is precisely what Dr. Boyer and Dr. Levine have done. Unless we are absolute monarchs or natural killers, we turn to the art of rhetoric, the art of pursuing the understandings that lurk behind our surface symbolic dis-agreements. We think about how our discourse in these areas works and about how it might be improved. We analyze our terms and look beneath our verbal surfaces, searching for common grounds from which we can then begin discoursing at a new and improved level.

In the ancient terminology of rhetoricians, we seek to discover the topics, the topoi, the places or locations on which, or *in* which, a shared inquiry can take place. Whatever conclu-sions we come to as we confer, we shall be practicing, well or badly, the arts of rhetoric. Whether we practice them well will depend only in part on the quality of the formal education we received in them, because our education—or miseducation—in rhetoric continues willy nilly after formal schooling.

In using the much abused term *rhetoric* to cover everything any of us say in this book, I know I take some risks. Rhetoric has always had a mixed press. When the International Society for the History of Rhetoric met in Madison, Wisconsin, in April 1981, one entire afternoon was scheduled for papers on the long history of *attacks* on rhetoric. But we do not have to go to history to discover that the term is suspect. At least nine out of ten references to it in the press today are unfavorable. In popular usage it generally refers to the sleazier branches of the arts of persuasion, often synonymous with bombast or verbal trickery or deliberate obfuscation. It is what we substitute for substantive action or genuine thought, what we fall back on when serious arguments are lacking. "Although the President's deeper purpose was concealed in the rhetoric, [he] sent a red hot message . . . in his speech last Wednesday." "But Miss Caruso dismissed Healey's statement as 'rhetoric' and vowed to bring in the second round of her proposed cuts." This is surely the standard usage.

You might then well say, "If *rhetoric* is such a bad word, why not just get rid of it and use the words stressed in the Carnegie essay, *symbol sharing?*" But it is not just the word that is debunked; it is what it stands for. "Reaction [to Mayor Byrne's announcement that she will move into the Cabrini-Green housing project] was mixed Saturday night, with many calling the move courageous but symbolic." Courageous — that's good. Symbolic, introduced with a *but* — that is obviously somehow bad, or at least inferior. "Alderman Danny Davis . . . said the move might be more symbolic than substantive." Obviously anything merely symbolic is not substantive, and if rhetoric is anything it is an employment of symbols.

If you detect a tone of defensiveness in these observations just think how you would feel if you professed a subject that gets itself talked about like that, every day, everywhere!

What people usually mean when they dismiss other people's efforts as "rhetoric" or, more often, "mere rhetoric" is that words or other symbols are being used to deceive or to obscure issues or evade action. Animals cannot tell elaborate lies, only simple ones. Animals cannot use symbols as evasion. Only a rhetoric-endowed species can produce an elaborate chain of lies to achieve a cover-up; or a multi-million dollar advertising campaign for products known to be either useless or harmful; or a diplomatic and political vocabulary for making the worse seem the better cause. Rhetoricians have often tried to wash their hands of such stuff, preserving the term rhetoric for cleaner varieties. But, as educators, we cannot accept that dodge. If we confer symbolic powers upon our students, we take on all of the risks of symbolic power. If we train our students in the arts of reading, writing, listening, and speaking, we shall inevitably empower them to do great harm in the world—to use rhetoric for private, antisocial ends, to break rather than build connections. I must return to this problem in a few moments, but, for now, perhaps we can simply label the whole domain of the deceitful rhetoric we deplore as "sub-rhetoric." Different people will probably have somewhat different examples in mind; hardly a day goes by without my adding to a list that exhibits, as its supreme moment, Richard Nixon's Checkers speech, when his family, and then his dog, won the hearts of a nation.

One step up from sub-rhetoric we find the word used to refer to the whole art of sincere selling of any cause, not just the trickery part or the disguise, but the genuinely persuasive parts too, including the logical arguments. In this sense, President Carter's rhetoric was said to be poor and President Reagan's is generally said to be good, meaning that, on average, people come away from their encounters with President Reagan having moved more or less in his direction. Almost every day we read that the United States must "improve its rhetoric throughout the world," obviously meaning "we must sell our case more effectively."

Though it is hard to distinguish this level of rhetoric, which I will call "mere rhetoric," from sub-rhetoric, obviously its uses can range from the most noble to the most dangerous, from Churchill's wartime speeches to the typical piece of campaign oratory. In some ways, mere rhetoric is more dangerous than sub-rhetoric because those who employ it are sincere; they have a position that they hope will prevail, and they themselves respect the rhetorical devices that they employ. Presidents Reagan and Carter both seem to believe in their hearts that they are good medicine for the country. More important to our analysis than their sincerity, however, is that they always give the impression of having used their rhetoric to put across a position that was known in advance, before the work on the rhetoric began. The case is already known: "OK, Sam, let's whomp us up some mere rhetoric to put it over. Let's see, who's our best ghost writer on this subject? George? OK, George, you know what we want, now get cracking on the rhetoric." The fact is that most freshman composition texts, even those that have taken up with the renewed fashion of using the word "rhetoric" in the title, imply that one's case is found by some other art or science, and then one puts it over with mere rhetoric.

Even if that were our final definition of the art, rhetoric would still obviously be indispensable in all general education, since its uses are shared by all who engage in any kind of practical endeavor. But it is hardly the art that I could bring myself to defend as what we should use in debating general education. Presumably, as we discuss our various proposals we do not think of ourselves as coming out of the discussion precisely as we came into it. We want to discover something through our rhetorical exchange.

As you know, Aristotle's own *Rhetoric* goes one large step further toward the definition we are seeking. Instead of being the art of persuasion about a case that is entirely known beforehand, rhetoric for Aristotle is the *faculty* or *capacity*, found of course *in the rhetorician, of discovering* or *inventing* "the possible means of persuasion in reference to any subject whatever." Unlike the arts of medicine, geometry, arithmetic (and presumably politics too, though Aristotle does not mention politics in this context), rhetoric "appears to be able to *discover* the means of persuasion in reference to any given subject." It is thus used by all disciplines, except insofar as those disciplines have available apodeictic proofs, what we call demonstrative or scientific proofs. Rhetoric in this view is not a dressing added to the case to make it persuasive; the rhetorician discovers the case itself, using the art of rhetoric as an art of discovery. When the search is successful, that case is persuasive, though the conclusions it leads to may not be true for all time and are certainly not demonstrated in any absolute sense.

This art, which I will call "rhetoric-B," is a marvel and a wonder. A scholar-teacher might honorably spend a whole career mastering its subtleties and passing the mastery along to students. Obviously it is a much more important subject than what most people call rhetoric. It will of course include the study of the inferior rhetorics — how otherwise could one distinguish the "bombast" and "empty verbal ornamentation" of one's enemies from the "true eloquence" and "sensitive verbal enrichments" of one's friends. But its true home will be what we call "value disputes" — in the political arena at its best, when a Pericles or a Lincoln or a Churchill reminds a nation of its deepest commitments; or in literary criticism; or in quarrels about the law or about constitutions. It comes into its own in every part of life where simple appeals to obvious facts or unquestioned logical proofs are not available — and that surely means most of what we do, even as scholars. Clearly, such a subject is immensely important, well worth the hundreds of pages of close study that Aristotle and Cicero gave it, and the many thousands that later students have added. There is nothing "mere" about it. It is the very lifeblood of our daily lives together.

But is it finally what we seek, if we are looking for the art of discovering and appraising the values we share? One obvious problem is that it seems to lack any limits on its power. Everyone who has thought hard about it has subordinated it to some other discipline, to make sure that it serves a higher good. It can be taught to villains as well as to saints, and it can be employed against the good of a society as well as for it. It is, of course, an immensely seductive art, because its mastery is the road to worldly success. (I am reminded of something a friend of mine said years ago. After a month or so teaching in a routine course called "Composition and Rhetoric" he lamented, "I feel as though I had been hired to stand at one side of the ladder of success and goose the little bastards as they climb.")

Rhetoric-B is the art of knowing what you want, and finding the really good arguments to win others to your side. It is the art of the good lawyer, of the effective business leader, of the successful fund raiser, and it is not to be scoffed at or ignored. But it does not itself teach us what ends it should serve; it is still an art without essential restraints other than those provided by the counterrhetoric created by other warriors or competitors. The world it builds, left on its own, is a world of a free market of atomized persons and ideas, each privately seeking victory and hoping that in the melee a public good will be produced by some invisible hand. Thus all thinkers from Plato and Aristotle on have felt the need to subordinate it to some higher discipline capable of revealing proper ends or goods. We see what happens when such higher controls are lacking, as various spokesmen for this or that new rhetorical theory — "communications skills," "propaganda analysis," "advertising techniques," "information science" — show themselves to be, in effect, available to the highest bidder: they fail to provide, from within themselves, any hint about limits to how and when their techniques are to be used.

But to what discipline or art now on the scene might we turn for the controls that each of our three kinds of rhetoric so clearly require? It takes no great skill in rhetoric to recognize that in our society at this time, there is open warfare about whether any superior "good" exists, or, if it does, what in fact it is and how it should be pursued. We seem to share no single notion of the good or of the proper methods of argument to be used in its pursuit.

If we did have such agreement, we could of course deduce from it proper uses of rhetoric: something like, "Service of the one true Lord requires, as Augustine teaches, that rhetoric should . . ." or "To restore our position as the world's greatest power, it is obvious that our rhetoric should. . . ." But we in America have agreed on something else instead—that we are to be a pluralistic society in which many different possible first principles will coexist. Some of them, like some scientists' and mathematicians' notions of what can be known, would rule out as trivial or non-cognitive most of the examples offered in the Carnegie essay. Some of them would suggest a list of co-ordinate values. And some, like mine, would lead to a more aggressive kind of hierarchical ordering, with certain threatened educational scandals seen as much more important than others.

When first principles conflict, how do we proceed? One possible way is to use rhetoric-B to persuade other people to change their minds and accept the predetermined *true* first principles. Marshalling all of the possible means of persuasion in our situation, we would, in that view, try to win as many converts as possible.

But did the Foundation's authors know, before they began to draft the report, not only how the report was to come out but how those who read and discuss it were supposed to respond? Did I know, as I began to write, what general education program we all should fight for on our campuses, using the best rhetoric we can muster?

Clearly, we all admire most another form of rhetoric entirely, one implied by my hierarchical progression from sub-rhetoric through mere-rhetoric and on to rhetoric-B namely — surprise! — a "rhetoric-A." When we are working together at our best, we repudiate both the autocratic imposition of a program by some benign dictator and the warfare of fixed positions; instead we try out our reasons on each other, to see where we might come out. We practice a rhetoric of inquiry.

To invent a label does not mean, of course, that the art we seek actually exists, and it certainly does not say that we will attain to it if it exists. But if there were an art that promised to aid us in going beneath the surface of our verbal disputes in order to discover the common values that underlie them and to build practical programs on them, would not mastery of that art be, for any pluralistic society, a noble art indeed?

Is there a rhetoric-A? Is there a supreme art of inquiry through symbols that is designed, not to win by cheating, as in sub-rhetoric, not merely to win sincerely, as in mere rhetoric, and not just to marshal all of the good reasons there might be for accepting what one knows already, but rather to discover and refine, in critical exchange, our ends, our purposes, our values?

Let me stress again the curious point that we have intuitively elected to practice that unnamed art whenever we engage in conferences that permit open exchange of ideas. What is more, I suspect that despite all our rhetorical faults as a nation, it remains true that no other society has ever committed itself so passionately to the search for rhetoric-A. Often this commitment is mocked, as people get impatient with committee work, with the cumbersomeness of representative government, with the absurdities of our thousands of national conventions, colloquia, conferences, workshops, and commissions. "Just think of all the time, energy, and money that is being wasted at this moment by hard working, intelligent people, who travel thousands of miles to confer together in muddle-headed fashion, using dubious arguments about unformulated questions, appealing to unclear principles and leading to ambiguous conclusions!"

Well, that's rhetoric-A for you! We seem to be stuck with it, not only when we confer in person but whenever we seriously take other people's views into account. So let us try for a somewhat clearer definition of this rhetoric that we seek to practice together when we are at our best.

Is it not *the art of appraising the warrants for assent in any symbolic exhange?*

The definition may seem anti-climactic until we think about the ground covered by its four key terms:

Appraising — the judging of the real validity or force, the power or weakness of something.

Warrants — the reason or motives given by one human being to another as support for some belief or action or change of mind (note that we move here beyond notions of "proof" or "demonstration." Such ostensibly hard stuff becomes only a subset of all the more or less good grounds we can give each other for changing our minds and hearts).

Assent — rather than dissent, because, though the two notions of saying "yes" and saying "no" are indissolubly linked in all human exchange, assent is really prior. Of the many reasons one might mention, the most obvious is that "thinking together about warrants" cannot even be undertaken without a primal act of assent: "I" must assent to "your" equal right to a hearing in our mutual endeavors; note again the contrast with traditional notions of hard proof, sought usually in private inquiry by disproving other people's views, and then imposed upon a reluctant world. What is more, the "I" who assents or dissents was long since constituted in a series of incorporations of other selves. Hence:

Symbolic exchange —like the other, inferior rhetorics, this one is indissolubly bound with the notion that it takes at least two to tango. But unlike the other definitions, this one rejects the very notion of the private individual "self" thinking by "itself." We move, instead to a kind of thought possible only for a radically social self of the kind Dr. Boyer has hinted at in saying that the dichotomy between the individual and his past is unreal. Good thinking in this view will not be quite like the "clear thinking" touted in so many handbooks of logic, something performed by the "individual" in opposition to all those sloppy thinkers "out there." Instead it will be "social thought" even when it is in some sense private; good thinking will be only that kind of thinking that takes into account what others have said or can say against it. And it will be, from first to last, richer than what could be said, or even thought, by any one party in the exchange.

It is clear that if there is such an art, it must include the skills of appraising arguments offered in the inferior kinds of rhetoric, and it must no doubt include the appraisal and placement of the various kinds themselves. In that sense, I have been trying to practice rhetoric-A throughout this essay. But rhetoric-A can be practiced in the simplest of exchanges — the argument with your neighbor over the smell of his gingko tree, the discussion with a student about a low grade, the debate in committee about whether to require competence in a foreign language. In fact, I want now to suggest that rhetoric-A is indeed the most general of all general arts, and that to neglect it in our general requirements, as, indeed, we too often do, is the most scandalous of all the scandals we perpetrate. I know that I can trust you to discount the outrageous arrogance in such a claim. I fully expect other disciplines to make similar moves—and I ask only that, when they do, we insist on real argument in their support, not just the claim that freshman courses are needed to attract majors. The best curricula will emerge, I am suggesting, when each of our imperialistic claims is forced into the courts of communal discourse, where our various rationalizations are transmuted, under critical scrutiny, into that special kind of reasoning I am calling rhetoric-A.

*T*o make my case, I must practice a bit of rhetoric-A on the notion of general education itself.

The trouble with all highly general terms like *general, shared,* and *connections,* is that, like *rhetoric,* they cover and sometimes even obscure essential distinctions. Some forms of generality are harmful—I offer the easy examples of totalitarian imposition of general aims and practices on a whole populace, and the soppy generalities offered by some "interdisciplinary" programs. Some sharings are dangerous—I cite only the exhilarated sharings that lead to mob action or national witch-hunts. Some connections are intellectually inhibiting—I cite only the ancient lumping of matter into the four elements, and the highly up-to-date and fashionable lumping of all narrative, including history, as "fictional" and therefore a form of lying. If we try to build our programs simply on what is shared or what is general, we shall be vulnerable to the first sophist who comes along and insists that we teach lying, just because all human beings lie; and proudful self-serving, just because all men and women are self-serving; and the arts of vandalism, just because scientific studies show that all of us share a capacity to take pleasure in destroying. In short, implicit in the Carnegie essay's emphasis on what is shared is a demand for distinctions of quality and kinds of generality. Once we limit ourselves to what we might call "generalities *worth having*," how many kinds do we find appealed to in the search for a general education? (Four of the following five kinds of generality, and the notion of distinguishing the four kinds, I borrow from that great student of rhetoric, Richard McKeon.)[1]

Education can be general in the sense of being generally shared by all students in a given setting. Many curricular planners have found themselves giving up on the hope for a reasoned selection of the knowledge most worth having. "Who can say that everybody must know a given Dickens novel rather than the great Chinese novel *Monkey*,[2] or Platonic thought rather than Zen Buddhism, or the second law of thermodynamics rather than how to do a regression analysis in statistics? Nobody. But we can say that it is good for students to share a culture, locally, so we'll make up a list of more-or-less arbitrary general requirements ensuring that they'll at least have some-

Common Learning

thing to talk about together." Rather minimal thinking, this, but no doubt better than nothing.

Education can be general, secondly, in the sense of covering the general needs of all citizens in a given time and place. That it should do so was the standard argument used by the defenders of the great Hutchins program of fourteen required year-long courses. Usually their talk was explicitly about preparation for citizenship. "We seek an education that all Americans should have, because it would be folly to expect anyone to exercise the choices presented by our society without having the fourteen competencies our comprehensive examinations cover. All citizens will have to exercise these competencies, regardless of what the future brings; therefore they should share a standard preparation in them."

A rather different curriculum emerges if we emphasize a third kind of general sharing, the methods and subject matters that all the genuine modes of inquiry share. Proponents of *"the scientific method"* have argued that all genuine thought depends on certain paradigms of proof, and that general education should build habits of thought that will be generally useful, in all fields, though obviously radically unshared by most citizens. Programs with emphasis on training in logic, semantics, linguistics, laboratory techniques, computer technology, and mathematics have emerged from such paradigms. They tend to show little concern about whether any two students have both read Shakespeare, or studied the Constitution, or thought about the role of law in public affairs, or developed skill in communicating their "scientific" results, or learned the same computer language.

Entirely different curricula have been suggested by proponents of a fourth notion of generality, based on what is common to all people in all cultures. "Our deepest connections are with humankind as a whole, and nothing is worse, educationally, than our chauvinistic concentration on western culture. What all students should learn are the experiences that join them to the rest of the world, not the narrow and elitist canons of western taste. What could be more absurd, in the modern world, than the western provincial who knows all about Beethoven and is ignorant of the Javanese gamelan?"

Finally, education can seek the general in the form of conceptual generalizations that serve as comprehensive over-reaching principles under which each discipline performs its work — whatever generalizes all particulars in a field or in all fields. Surely if there is some "general field theory" it should be our center. Many mathematicians and physical scientists have pursued a truly general truth that could provide a capstone for all knowledge. As Morris Kline has recently said, mathematics offers all the values offered by any field, and, in addition, is "the paradigm for the best knowledge available."[3] For certain religious planners, on the other hand, it has seemed obvious that an education without a knowledge of God as a capstone is not education at all but a misapprehension of fragments. "Surely an education that does not lead the student to try to put it all together, to see not just connections but the ultimate connectedness, can hardly be considered really general, and it is not worthy of being required."

*A*t first consideration, this list of rival sharings may seem daunting. Regardless of where we would place our own planning, or that of the Carnegie Foundation, we are all aware that there are these rival views — that the shambles the report rightly deplores comes in part from the failure of educators to think through which of these notions of the general they are pursuing, and why. All five build in a rejection of trivial or base kinds of sharing. But are all versions of each of them equally important?

On another occasion I would like to pursue these complexities and to discover where each of these notions would lead us if we asked not simply whether a given learning would be nice to have, but whether it should be required for all students. But here, I can only report my daunting discovery that I am unwilling to give up any of the five. Though it is easy to see how special versions of each can be in direct competition with the others, it is obvious that each is radically desirable, in the precise sense that we began with: there is a kind of scandal in giving the BA to any student who has no common intellectual bonds with other students, with all other citizens, with all genuine disciplines, with all human cultures, and with all who seek to discover truths that are truly general.

If all five kinds are desirable, we can then begin to play an interesting game. Which of the many sharings on the Carnegie report's list, all of them good things to have, can make the best case for itself as indispensable, according to one or more of the notions of generality?

Again I shall, of course, leave it to others to make their cases for disciplines other than rhetoric. But I would not be doing my duty by an ancient and honorable discipline if I did not claim that rhetoric-A, the development of the appraisal (and hence the skillful use) of warrants for assent in human exchange is an art unrivaled in its service to all five kinds of general education. I hasten to add that it is an art that need not be taught under the title of "rhetoric." You may prefer to call it "dialectic," or "philosophy of discourse," or "practical discourse," as we do in our undergraduate program at the University of Chicago, PERL — Politics, Economics, Rhetoric, Law. I cannot think of any course in which some contribution to its mastery could not be made, if a teacher really tried. But it is too easily neglected when it is not given a clear and distinctive place in the curriculum; and when it is neglected, all the other disciplines suffer.

In the first place, and perhaps most obviously, if students on a given campus are to share educational experience, whether imposed through requirements or discovered simply by living together, they will do so largely in their use of rhetoric, good or bad. Only to the degree that they learn to practice rhetoric-A, appraising together the warrants for assent that they and their teachers and texts offer, will they learn what to share and what not to share, what positions to buy and what to reject. In short, rhetoric is the very medium in which students share most of their genuine education, including most of their classroom experiences in the hardest of the sciences. The rhetoric may very well be of inferior kinds; even the best teachers may find occasional uses for hamming, tear-jerking, blood-letting, and swinging from the chandeliers. But surely our ideal of education is the sharing of *good* reasons for changes of mind, and since in most subjects that we care about there are no rigorous mathematical or experimental proofs available even for the simplest processes and conclusions, our hope must lie in rhetoric-A. (On another occasion it would be useful to show that even the hardest of the sciences cannot prove scientifically their basic assumptions, and must depend, when dealing with those assumptions, on rhetoric-A.)

It seems equally obvious, secondly, that the primary need of all citizens, before, during, and after college graduation, is a mastery of rhetoric. The business of American life is, after all, conducted—perhaps more than was true of any previous society

—*in* rhetoric. Unlike people in traditional societies, we get our jobs, keep them or lose them, and actually conduct them, with rhetoric. *The Chronicle of Higher Education* has recently made the claim that more than 50 percent of all Americans make their living at what the *Chronicle* elegantly calls "symbol pushing." You would think, then, that every college in this practical land would have at least one entire degree program in how to symbol-push better than other symbol pushers. But if you have such a program on your campus, one that goes beyond the mere rhetoric of advertising skills, I shall be surprised, and I hope to learn about it. I shall be even more surprised if your catalogues list more than one required general course that might conceivably be named "Improved Symbol-Pushing 101."

Rhetoric as vocational training is obviously far more important than we recognized. But I would stress even more strongly its value in serving our universal need for *political* savvy. All our political life, except what is done through bribery and violence, is conducted in one or another form of rhetoric. Working together in symbolic exchange is in fact our only alternative to tyranny; either someone will impose forms of life upon us, or we must learn to embrace forms of life by trying them out on each other. And if we cannot manage to do the trying out effectively, if we cannot rise above sub- and mere- and B-rhetorics to an effective appraisal of our reasonings, we are doomed to some form of chaos, inevitably followed by some tyrant's takeover.

Our founding fathers did the trying out at a wonderfully high level; my students and I have been discovering just how high as we work over the rhetoric-A of Madison's *Notes* and the rhetoric-B of *The Federalist Papers*, in that new program I mentioned, "PERL." (The Founders were highly skilled in the use and analysis of the lower rhetorical forms, too; what we might call our founding uncles, like Tom Paine, owed their astonishing popular success to a rhetorical range that any of us might envy.) What is more, every generation since then has offered its demonstration that unless effective rhetoric governs politics, money and violence will. The Constitution in this view is a marvelously shrewd effort to guarantee that rhetoric will have a chance — an effort to open up public spaces that will require, not just allow, that our many different would-be governors listen to each other and listen to the governed. The fact that we survive at all as a democracy is a triumph of that great piece of rhetoric-A — and of our willingness to talk and listen according to its rules.

If there is only one alternative to the brute force of bribery or threatened violence you would expect study of that alternative to be the required center of every plan for democratic education. What we find instead are hundreds of colleges that do not require even one year of training in how to read, write, speak, or listen, and thousands of major programs in which students never do any significant writing of their own or analyze anyone else's arguments carefully. I invite you, with some anguish, to take a close look, when you return to your own campus, at the textbooks now being used there.

Thirdly, rhetoric is general to all disciplines, in the sense of their depending on it in daily practice. Though many disciplines are described as if rhetoric were beneath their high-minded endeavors, one has only to look at the rhetoric used in the field itself, both in its publications and its teaching practice, to see the absurdity of the claim. The fact is that every field depends, often in surprising degrees, on the skills I am talking about.

I will not insist, as some rhetoricians have done, on the claim that even the hardest proofs in the hardest sciences are conducted *in* rhetoric: "the rhetoric of the laboratory," "the rhetoric of the equation," "the rhetoric of the graph." But even if we grant the name of pure science to the processes of decisive and final demonstration, we know that most of the business of scientists, even when they are writing in their front-line journals, depends on obviously rhetorical arguments like exploration of hidden or overt analogies, colorful metaphor, appeals to the character of the speaker and of supporting institutions, and direct or subtle manipulation of readers' emotions. We should not have needed *The Double Helix*,[4] or *Lucy*,[5] the new book purporting to reveal how anthropologists work, to teach us what a small portion of every scientist's scientific life is decided by scientific evidence.

The infusion of rhetoric, of our kinds of reasons, good and bad, is usually not noticed, especially when it comes in the form of appeals to certain root metaphors that everyone in the field simply takes for granted. When it is noticed it is usually treated as a kind of impurity that would be washed away if only scientists were more scientific. But rhetoric is inescapable, even in mathematics and physics, to say nothing of all the other fields hinted at in the Carnegie report's list of sharings. Leaving aside the obvious rhetoric of the grant proposal and the seminar room, a very large part of what every inquirer in every field says in "scientific" debate with colleagues is not backed with certain proof. As Michael Polanyi[6] has shown, in his great book *Personal Knowledge*, no scientist could ever prove scientifically most of the scientific beliefs he or she accepts. In every science, scientists believe most of what they believe about it—all except their own very tiny specialist's domain — without even being able to follow, in detail, the proofs that other specialists would offer. This does not mean that they believe their colleagues on what is called "blind faith." They believe their colleagues because they have more or less reliable warrants for assent of the kind that rhetoricians have always studied. For example, nobody has ever decisively disproved, and nobody could conceivably disprove, any of the wild popular assertions of pseudoscience, the theories of Velokovsky or van Daniken, the experiments of hordes of para-psychologists, the reports of UFOlogists and what not. Yet all scientists of repute reject these schemes by the dozens, annually, without investigation; life would be intolerable for them if they did *not* reject them *without scientific investigation,* trusting to rhetorical warrants like authority, emotional commitment to "the scientific method," and pure hunch. On the other hand, all scientists accept dozens of new developments annually in fields outside their specialties, on grounds that can only be called rhetorical: the strength of personal and communal warrants that have nothing to do with scientific proof. Since such warrants never yield certainty, the people who make these choices sometimes turn out to have been wrong; occasionally a "wild" scheme later establishes itself and an established truth is overthrown. But most of what we think of as scientific life would simply disappear if such uncertainties led scientists to insist on scientific proofs for every belief on which they act.

Unfortunately, it is impossible to exhibit here the kind of field-by-field survey that would be required to support my claim that rhetoric is essential to and practiced in all disciplines. Short of a complete demonstration of how all learning depends on rhetoric, I must be content with the simple reminder of how much every scientist relies on it. I am not thinking only of effective popularizations of the kind that Lewis Thomas practices so well. I am thinking rather of the fact that whenever any inquirer chooses to address anyone except other advanced inquirers in a given field, rhetoric comes into its own.

In a longer version of this paper I have looked at an

extensive verbatim account of a group of economists debating a colleague's paper. What are their procedures? They consist, for the most part, of rhetoric-B, occasionally rising to rhetoric-A. You may think economists are too easy a mark—after all, none of us watching the recent TV series done by Milton Friedman had the illusion that what he was practicing, with those shots of happy workers in Hong Kong sweatshops, was the *science* of economics. But consider, then, as representative of what plays a necessary part in every field, the kind of thing one finds in *Scientific American.* That wonderful journal brings a hazy sense of scientific developments to us laymen, but what is interesting is that it also provides, as I learn in talking to scientific colleagues, many of the beliefs that scientists themselves hold about sciences other than their own. Not long ago one could read the following:

The first test of Einstein's general theory of gravitation to be made on objects outside the solar system was reported shortly before the 100th anniversary of Einstein's birth. The opportunity for such a test presented itself with the discovery in 1974 of a radio pulsar that is a member of a binary pair ... PSR1913 +16. Since 1974 the signal emitted by PSR1913 +16 has been closely monitored by its codiscoverer, Joseph H. Taylor of the University of Massachusetts at Amherst, with the 305-meter radio telescope at Arecibo in Puerto Rico. In a recent issue of Nature *Taylor ... report[s] the results of some 1000 observations over four years. With gradual improvement in technique pulse-arrival time can now be established with an accuracy of about 50 microseconds.*[7]

Like wow! Little did I dream! Yet it must be true. *One thousand* observations! 50 *microseconds! Closely* monitored! At U. Mass! Reported in *Nature!* All of this is, of course, rhetoric, mere rhetoric.

There follow three paragraphs of explanation, at a highly

general level. In a state of happy, easy faith, I go on to the next item: "How Interferon Interferes." The conclusions of that one I also accept, sort of, because "the remarkable ability of the protein interferon to inhibit the multiplication of viruses in animal cells has tantalized biochemists and virologists ever since its discovery in 1957," and also because a scientist from *The University of California*(!) at Santa Barbara, no less, has reported his work in *The Proceedings of the National Academy of Sciences*! Rhetoric. Not terribly good warrants here, once I think about them. Not good enough to satisfy me, especially if I am an astronomer or virologist. But we can be sure that every mathematician, say, or economist, who reads this will tentatively add this lore, as I do, to "what science has proved."

Since I am aware of how far my evidence here falls short of my vast generalization, perhaps I can just appeal to your own expertise. Simply think of the last article you read in your own field, one not addressed to the general public, and then ask, what proportion of the propositions in it that you accept could *you* yourself prove or disprove according to Karl Popper's criterion of falsifiability,[8] as the model of how scientists think. My guess is that the figure will run as low as 5 percent. There is absolutely nothing wrong in that — except when poor education in the intellectual procedures needed for that remaining 95 percent leaves people floundering.

I can do even less justice to the fourth kind of sharing—our connections with all cultures, all of humankind. It is perhaps self-evident that rhetoric in some form will be found in all cultures. The capacity to engage in symbolic exchange, the capacity to use statements about the world rather than mere pointing or brute force, is recognized by all anthropological schools as a distinctive feature—perhaps the essential feature— of human cultures. Though what constitutes a good reason, a genuine warrant, will vary considerably from culture to culture, I can be sure in advance of studying any new culture that people in it will have their own way of distinguishing good argument from bad, and they will recognize a difference between those who are good at finding the right words and those whose words mislead or destroy. I can be equally sure that any chance we have of building understanding among cultures will depend on a rhetoric of discovery. What do we share beneath our surface differences? Let us inquire together, in symbolic exchange. There is no other way except to eliminate differences by forceful domination.

So I must assume, without adequate argument, that rhetoric is a universally needed and practiced art, if there is any such thing as a universally needed and practiced art, hurrying on to the fifth and most implausible of all my claims today. Most traditional educational systems have sought to study and instill understanding of some kind of ultimate good, some supreme standard against which all of our interests and endeavors can be measured. We today can rely on no such standard. We know that our culture has no publicly acknowledged and universally accepted ultimate standard of that kind. Our question then becomes: Can rhetoric in any sense fill a gap that is left when theology, philosophy, the idea of scientific progress, faith in ultimate political revolution, and all other gods have failed?

To show how it might do so would be a tall order, even if I had more space. I can only suggest that when we ask the question, "What warrants for assent are *really* good ones?" we are forced to practice rhetoric-A at the highest possible level—one that indeed we may want another name for: meta-rhetoric, perhaps, or rhetorology? We are then asking the kind of question that the Carnegie essay calls for when it asks us to think about the "issues of values that we share in common." We are pushing ourselves to reflect not just on the warrants for assent in particular cases, but on the ultimate ways of grounding assent, the varieties of modes of assenting, modes of warranting.

The rhetorologist will be interested not so much in whether Mr. A. or Mr. B. wins in a particular debate, or even *how* they win or lose, as in the structures of assumption and proof that both share, and in how these structures might differ from the structures found in neighboring disciplines, or in the same discipline a decade before or a decade after. You can see immediately that there are a lot of rhetorologists around, traveling under other names. Indeed in most disciplines these days one finds people who are reopening "settled" questions about what constitutes good warrants for assent in that discipline—they are exploring the ways we think about the ways we think. One sees efforts everywhere to rehabilitate proofs that earlier thinkers tried to reject: "telling a good story" as one form of validation in history; analogy as one form of genuine argument in science; metaphor as inescapable in all inquiry; the persuasive force of a speaker's ethos; appeals to tradition or precedent; even a legitimated and controlled reliance on emotional stirrings.

Even more important than the critical rehabilitation of these warrants rejected by earlier positivisms is the critical probing of basic assumptions within and among the disciplines. Suddenly everyone seems to be aware that human thought does not have to be either strictly deductive or strictly empirical but can be "topical," rhetorical. If you look at any statement that purports to be proof, in any discipline, you find that it relies on "unprovable" assumptions, sometimes stated, often left tacit: assumptions about what makes a fact in that subject; about the purpose of inquiry; about the self-evidence of certain principles and definitions; about the proper methods of moving back and forth between "unquestioned" principles and "undeniable" facts. The work of the rhetorologist is precisely to pursue the comparative worth of different warrants in different persuasive enterprises, and to invent — or if you prefer, discover — improved ways for minds to meet within disciplines and among seemingly different or conflicting disciplines.

To the rhetorician—though not to most other people—it has been clear for more than 2000 years that none of the individual disciplines provides a method for examining the basic assumptions necessary to the practice of that method. The lawyer does not use legal argument to establish the validity of legal argument; to do that requires some kind of political philosophy—either one derived from an established authority or good, like the divine right of kings, or one that is discovered in symbolic intercourse among those who choose to think about such matters — that is, by rhetorology. The physicist cannot prove, using the methods of physical science, even that nature exists, or that the proofs of physics are any more than game playing, or that evidence should not be fudged, and so on. Rhetorologists cannot "prove" such matters either, and they welcome what might be called the "Gödel bandwagon,"[9] that new growth industry convincing even the mathematicians that *ultimate, certain* proofs are not to be had. The rhetorologist has always known what popularizers of Gödel are saying, that "truth" is a larger concept than "proof," that there are many truths that are "uncertifiable." For rhetorology this has never presented a crisis but simply a challenge to find new topics, new shared places from which any given rhetorical community can move, trusting to various degrees of warranting in the search for liveable truths, not certainties.

As I reminded you earlier, most philosophies have hoped to school the vagaries of various rhetorics, to rein in the immensely frisky pony of mankind's free-ranging symbols, by discovering some supreme single substance or method that all could — or should — adhere to; some metaphysics or meta*some*thing that could determine which first principles are *really* first and then estblish the others in relation to it. There are of course many thinkers today who still pursue that kind of hope for a supreme monistic view of all knowledge. But I don't have to tell you that they move in many different paths to many different ultimate principles. And as soon as they offer to take us with them to their heights, as soon as they attempt to meet those of us who do not share a self-evident vision of some single ordered truth, they perforce must enter the domains of rhetoric—either the lower forms, attempting to win converts; or rhetorology, attempting to discover common ground between their programs and ours. Thus even those who hold to a faith that someday, somehow, a unified language of all knowledge will be discovered, with a universally accepted supreme substance or concept to validate it, are forced to work here and now in a pluralistic world of differences that are not found just on the surface but that run very deep, a messy world of dispute, of lines of reasoning that are only probable, not certain, of major questions about which there seem to be not just two sides but many sides.

In that world some people become skeptical and even cynical: if nothing can be finally demonstrated, everything is equally doubtful; all claims to knowledge are spurious. But the rhetorologist has learned, from practicing the less comprehensive kinds of rhetoric, that to be uncertain is not the same as to be cognitively helpless. Having learned to use symbolic exchange to test the "maybes" in everyday affairs, the rhetorologist is not afraid to use such exchange to test the maybes that we dispute "at the top," as it were. The faith required to do so is not a blind faith, because it is perpetually rewarded with islands of clarity that make human life not only possible but rewarding. It will look like blind faith only to those who insist that there is only one kind of serious inquiry — the pursuit of certainty; all the rest is mere guesswork, *mere* rhetoric.[10]

Clearly I have thrown caution to the winds and allowed my imperialism to run riot. My claim is not of course that those other good things on the Carnegie list should be discarded; in any college curriculum I could respect, all would be pursued vigorously. But I do fear that the essay's careful rhetorology, its search for what we share beneath our differences of expression, may become quickly corrupted, when it gets in the hands of curriculum committees, corrupted into a list of six or eight required courses. Then, when the committee report is manhandled by the faculty council, the final new plan, to be hailed in *The New York Times* or *Time* magazine, as the product of the Carnegie Foundation study, will cut the eight courses to four: one called Freshman English, the rest turned into distribution requirements in history, the social sciences, and the natural sciences. Category six, our shared values, the study of ethics, will simply be dropped, as it almost always is, as too hot to handle. If we are to forestall that mutilation, we must push ourselves into thinking hard about what specific priorities we share, and about how to answer, and about how to train our students to answer, when some Ned Snyder pronounces, "Gentlemen, we are already the best men's college in the country. Why on earth should we change . . . ?"

Well, that is one kind of rhetorical flourish with which I might well end. But since in these muddy waters one inevitably feels a bit desperate, I cannot resist trying again.

When Matthew Arnold was about to go to Oxford, his father, Thomas, wrote to the University to ask whether Aristotle's *Rhetoric* was required study there. "I could not," he said, "consent to send my son to [a] University where he would lose it altogether." Many, perhaps most, of our students, "lose it altogether," and I rather doubt that many parents of your students have threatened to withdraw them because of the lack. What they may complain about, these days, is the failure of the college to teach "the basics." Obviously, then, our problem is in one sense quite simple: just teach the public the truth, namely that what they mean when they cry "back to the basics!" is "Back to rhetoric!"

With such efforts at resounding peroration I dramatize that my program is circular: we must use a corrupted medium to improve that medium. But the circularity does not alarm me, because it need not be vicious. A vicious circle is actually a spiral, moving downward. Sometimes rhetoric, especially political rhetoric, does work like that. But we have all experienced moments when the spiral moved upward, when one party's effort to listen and speak just a little bit better, produced a similar response, making it possible to try a bit harder —and on up the spiral to moments of genuine understanding.

NOTES

1. McKeon, Richard. "The Battle of the Books" in Booth, Wayne (ed.) *The Knowledge Most Worth Having* (Chicago, The University of Chicago Press, 1967) pp. 188-189.

2. Wu-Ch'Eng-En. *Monkey, Folk Novel of China,* translated by Arthur Waley (New York, Grove Press, 1958). The complete classic from which Waley's work is excerpted is now available in English for the first time as *The Journey to the West,* translated by Anthony Yu (Chicago, The University of Chicago Press, vol. 1, 1977; vol. 2, 1978; vol. 3, 1981; vol. 4, forthcoming).

3. Kline, Morris. *Mathematics: The Loss of Certainty* (New York, Oxford University Press, 1980).

4. Watson, James D. *The Double Helix: A Personal Account of the Discovery of the Structure of DNA* (New York, Atheneum, 1968).

5. Johanson, Donald, and Edey, Maitland. *Lucy* (New York, Simon and Schuster, 1981).

6. Polanyi, Michael. *Personal Knowledge: Toward a Post-Critical Philosophy* (Chicago, The University of Chicago Press, 1958. Harper Torchbook, 1964). See especially ch. 9, "The Critique of Doubt."

7. *Scientific American,* May 1979, pp. 82, 86, 90.

8. Popper, Karl R. *The Logic of Scientific Discovery* (London, Hutchinson, 1959. Rev. 1968). See especially chs. 4-6.

9. The best account, for the nonmathematician, of the revolution affected by Gödel's famous paper of 1931 is offered by Nagel, Ernest, and Newman, James R. in *Gödel's Proof* (New York, New York University Press, 1958). Some hint of the uses the proof can be made to serve in popularizations of science can be seen in the delightful best seller, Douglas R. Hofstadter, *Gödel, Escher Bach: An Eternal Golden Braid* (New York, Basic Books, 1979).

10. It is not appropriate to my argument to lay down the principles that I expect to be found by rhetorologists who think together long and hard about the grounds of their discourse. But one thing is clear from recent probings in various fields: metaphysical questions that many modernists thought settled once and for all, settled with firm answers like "God is dead" or "Values are man-made and therefore nonrational," are now reopened. The ancient "proofs for the existence of God," for example, had been shown to carry no rigorous "scientific force." But they are coming alive again, sometimes in traditional vocabulary, sometimes in entirely new terms. See, for example, Iris Murdoch's *The Sovereignty of Good* (London, Routledge & Kegan Paul, 1970).

Heritage and Traditions

BY FREDERICK RUDOLPH

CHAPTER THREE

*H*enry Ford gave us the moving assembly line and an automobile designed, engineered, and priced for mass consumption. He also made notable contributions to the "sayings of great men." "I don't like to read books, they mess up my mind" is one of them. Another: "I wouldn't give five cents for all the art in the world." The one that strikes near the heart of this essay is a brief and uncompromising judgment on history, issued in response to a question posed by a reporter from the *Chicago Tribune* in 1919. Ford had taken the *Tribune* to court over some allegedly libelous judgments of its own. He won the case, but the trial was an embarrassing ordeal in which the man's ignorance titillated the nation.

Ford did not help matters when he said to the *Tribune* reporter: "History is more or less bunk," but apparently the drift of national sentiment in the schools and colleges has been much in Ford's favor. My purpose, after all these years, is, if not to refute the wizard of Dearborn, at least to present a case for a concern with the past as an essential element in the learning of all people.

The first time that I was called upon to represent the claims of history was about thirty years ago when, fresh out of graduate school, I was asked by my chairman to give the opening lecture in the freshman course in the history of Western civilization, known in those simple days as History 1-2. That lecture was by tradition the responsibility of Phinney Baxter, the president of the college, but he was out of town, and the opportunity fell to me, I assume, because, as the most recent recruit to the department, I might offer the freshest observations.

Whatever may have been said on that occasion, no record of it remains in my files. I am, therefore, unable to contrast what surely must have been the enthusiasms, the hopes, the assumptions of a young historian with the experiences and conclusions of one who is on the eve of retirement. I do recall telling the freshmen that the study of history would protect them from being misled by *Time* magazine, but that did not take fifty minutes.

In any case, now, thirty years later, we do know that the comfortable curricular structures and assumptions of an earlier day no longer support the historian in his effort to justify attention to the past. The past has not altogether been thrown away, but somewhere along the line its relevancy came to be questioned, other excitements crowded in upon it, and the oppressive demands of the present, of the NOW, took over. We sense an incompleteness in the college graduate whose sense of self is uninformed by a sense of the connections that unite people, that make past and present and future a dynamic continuum, and that put into perspective the inheritance and traditions that shape our daily lives. We who teach history find ourselves reading student papers and historical essays that lack respect for specificity and chronology, as if they did not matter, as if the relationships that derive from time, sequence, and place in the past could not possibly be very important in the present and future.

Lurking in our uneasiness is, I suspect, a yearning for the return of what was known in nineteenth-century institutions of higher education as "the whole man," a desire to recapture that wholeness and completeness, the comprehensiveness and symmetry, that once characterized (or was thought to) a college education. Now, there is nothing wrong with a bit of nostalgia in one's life, but it can be a very troublesome guide to the future. Unlike history, which may lead a student to an understanding of tragedy as a human condition, nostalgia is pure romance. As much as we might wish, therefore, that today's graduate might go out into the world with those qualities of character and culture that denoted the whole man of the classical course of study, a few words of caution are in order.

In the nineteenth century, the philosophers and guardians of the concept of the whole man—I fear that there were not yet any whole women — described his antithesis as fiends, vile creatures, eviscerated grinning skeletons, mere fractions of men. It is actually such alternatives to the generally educated man and woman that we have in mind when we deplore the disarray and fragmentation that have overtaken the curriculum in the past 100 years. Our language is less colorful, but we know that we are haunted by the fear, and sometimes the evidence, that, instead of turning out educated men and women, we may be casting loose on society generations of barbarians. Before we are done in by our fears, however, let us take a look at that whole man.

It is true that he did not possess sufficient knowledge or understanding of anything in particular that would have allowed him to be considered narrowly expert, or unbalanced. He could not be judged by his usefulness, because he did not know enough about anything to be useful. And he was utterly lacking in the resources—the skepticism, respect for the accidental, the flexibility, the sense of ambiguity, contradiction, and paradox—that informed and supported intellectual power.

The whole man was not judged by what he knew (the old curriculum did not really allow him to know very much; the sciences, history, the social studies, literature since the ancients, art, music, the modern languages made their way into the equipment of an educated person as beneficiaries of the elective system that destroyed the old curriculum). But if the whole man was not to be judged by his knowledge, there was no question about whether he could be judged by his culture and character. The ultimate test of the educated man, of the whole man, was not whether he was informed or whether he was bright, but whether he was good.

Yet, as you and I know, it is not enough to be good. The trouble with the whole man was that he was so thoroughly indoctrinated in the beliefs and spirit of the Puritan tradition that he himself was at war with the compelling movements of the time—material progress and political democracy. His belief in an educated class of standardbearers of culture, taste, and morality, of which he was a representative, rested on the assurances provided him by his Calvinist faith, the authority of the classical curriculum, and access to the professions and good society provided by the baccalaureate degree.

All that changed, and that is why imagination and great energies seem to be engaged in an endless quest for a curriculum that, while acknowledging the change, will provide direction and opportunities appropriate to the perceived needs of the individual and society. It is not necessary to recapitulate the entire history of American higher education in order to understand that the local, regional, and national elites fashioned by the nineteenth-century colleges and universities were elites quite different from those being developed on our campuses today, and light years in distance of purpose and style from the mass enrollments that now account so much for what a college education is. Nor is it necessary to hanker after the return of that earlier elite, with all of its weaknesses, in order to admit that we all would be better off if somehow we could capture some of its better qualities and purposes and transfer them to the future.

If we cannot reverse history, however, surely we can try to understand why we as a people are where we are today. Looking back at the century just passed and forward to the decades ahead, assessing the accelerating changes that beset the modern world, Henry Adams, in the final pages of his celebrated *Education* came to the urgent conclusion that "thus far, since five or ten thousand years, the mind had successfully reacted, and nothing yet proved that it would fail to react — but it would need to jump."[1] Adams's tribute to intellectual power and authority says something about what happened to the whole man and the class of which he was a part, to the clients and supports of the old curriculum. Their minds reacted, but they failed to jump. Their values were sound; indeed, they *were* very good men, but they essentially constituted the core of local, regional, and national aristocracies that were in process of decline and displacement, being shunted aside by vigorous generations of democratically recruited and materialistically motivated young men and women, eager to prove their usefulness to society, to solve its problems, and lead their professions in the application of knowledge and power. A meritocracy was in the making.

If in these candidates for a meritocratic elite we recognize young men and women for whom we would provide a common learning, perhaps also we will be prepared to distinguish them and their predecessors in other ways as well. For, however ready I may be to fault the whole man for his shallowness and intellectual weakness, even for his snobbishness, I am equally certain that he was secure in his knowledge of himself, that his curricular and extracurricular experiences provided him with many common avenues of access to an understanding of the meaning of being human, encouraging him to take stock of who he was, where he came from, what he stood for, where he was going. I do not believe that the same is true of the young men and women who fill our colleges and universities today, who are being prepared to assume positions of leadership in our society and, on Henry Adams's terms, to meet the challenges of our time not by routine reaction but with great leaps of intellectual and moral imagination.

They may be preoccupied with self in a superficial way, in various hedonistic gratifications, in sex, in all this endless running and jogging that will some day be a source of wonderment and bewilderment to historians attempting to understand our culture. But they are essentially in too great a hurry to be on their way, too impatient to get under their belts the soon-to-be outdated technical knowledge essential to their material advancement, to have time and interest enough to search out their hearts and souls and psyches and the influences that have shaped them for the most important information of all: Who am I? Why am I? Where did I come from? Where am I going?

To recover the central importance of these questions for the curriculum and for the health of society is the great challenge that confronts those who are burdened with responsibility for the course of study. Knowledge, power, utility—these are easily imparted and eagerly sought, but unless they are applied by men and women who both understand their own uniqueness and comprehend the bonds that unite them, society will indeed be at the disposal of well-trained barbarians, knowledgeable technicians lacking the most essential knowledge of all.

A young man of my acquaintance startled me recently with his complaint that his college education was mired in the past, characterized by a nodding recognition of the present and a total disregard of the future. His description was so contrary to my own understanding that I was forced to explore the reasons that our perceptions were so far apart. It is altogether too easy to blame all of our discontents on television, but I am usually willing to begin there. In no way have I been educated by a television set, but it has been a very long time since I have had a student of whom the same might be said. My guess is that whatever we do in class, whatever we read, whatever our purpose, appears to the young to be mired in the past because it lacks the immediacy, the freshness, the breathlessness and drama of even the tamest of television programs. A student's sense of time is not shaped by a grasp of the moving forces of change, both slow and sudden, both predictable and unexpected, but by the accumulated instruction in the meaning of time that bit by bit is imparted by disconnected, unexplained, superficially organized information that has but a momentary life of its own. Everything is impermanent, fleeting.

In contrast, whatever may be happening in class appears heavy, substantial—in the past, as it were, even though nothing of a historical nature or understanding may be going on at all. There is no reason why a program called "Today" should be about "Yesterday," but as an instrument for clarifying change, explaining relationships, developing an understanding of continuity and discontinuity in history, it is altogether subversive. Television does not intend to be subversive, but because, in Emerson's words, mankind is as lazy as it dares to be, television is a powerful force for encouraging passivity instead of vitality, acquiescence instead of questioning, simplicity instead of complexity. It poses as authority in matters about which its knowledge and understanding are at best elementary. It doesn't have the time for time.

To such influences I attribute some, but certainly not all, of my young acquaintance's misperceptions. If he doesn't know that he was studying the future, whatever else was happening, some of the responsibility must lie with himself, some with his instructors, for any classroom of young people *is* the future, and if that very obvious connection remains a secret, then what indeed is being studied is a matter of some mystery. Neither the past nor the present nor the future is delivered to our comprehension by itself alone. Indeed, history — the inquiry into what has gone before—opens the way to the future by enabling us to understand the past as a "key to the understanding of the present." John Donne's admonition presses on us: "No man is an island, entire of itself. . . . Everyman is a piece of the continent, a part of the main." In the very same sense, no man is of the present alone, he is neither emancipated from the past, nor free of a future that has not yet happened.

Yet, so complicated a view of man is peculiarly contrary to the ethos that has informed and shaped American culture. It is possible to argue that history belongs in the common curriculum, and in the course of my remarks I intend to suggest some not particularly original reasons why indeed it should be, but at the very beginning it is important to understand that, as a people, we have often lived, thought, and acted as if the past were dispensable.

I doubt if we can overestimate the significance of the origins and development of this country as a nation of immigrants and the role of that experience in shaping our view of the past. As an environment for new beginnings, the New World, then the Colonies, and finally the United States have called forth the energies and aspirations of men and women most ready and willing to uproot themselves, to discard the past, and to create for themselves new identities. Painful and difficult as these experiences may have been, they involved a rejection of the past, a not always acknowledged insistence that all that mattered had not yet happened. During his travels in the United States in the 1830s Alexis de Tocqueville was filled with amazement by the abandon with which Americans thrust upon him documents, state papers, and other material that belonged in safekeeping in national or other appropriate archives. But the Americans, much to Tocqueville's astonishment, were literally throwing the past away.

Not only did immigrants throw out their pasts as so much unwanted baggage, but the impulses to conformity in a democratic society and the stress on acculturation and assimilation tended to eliminate diversity, complexity, and ethnicity in favor of a bland and simple version of the past. For a very long time the past was served up as a succession of good Puritans, bad Indians, adventurous self-made men like Benjamin Franklin, Daniel Boone, and Thomas Edison, and whether one was black or white, man or woman, rich or poor, this was the only past one was asked to share or understand.

History has also been handicapped as an instrument of human understanding in the United States because the national culture has celebrated the importance of individualism, mobility, achieving, success—those qualities and experiences that are destructive of time and place and that substitute movement for stability. In America, it has often seemed, both for the individual and society itself, that nothing is stationary long enough to have a past. I am reminded of the New Yorker who, asked by a stranger whether this was Park Avenue, replied: "It used to be." Impermanence is one message that our self-destruction of cities delivers, but another is a contempt for heritage, continuity, and tradition.

Moreover, the cult of informality and the thrust of equalitarianism, as appropriate and understandable as they may be in a democratic society, are hostile to the institutions, practices, classes, traditions, and forms that support, inform, and define a sense of history. On an American college campus, anything that happens two years in a row is called a tradition; almost anything that happens three years is not likely to happen a fourth.

A pervasive innocence, both attractive and annoying, once held most Americans in its grasp. Compounded of an enduring faith in God and in nature's bounty and a simple belief in unassisted human effort, it confronted the future with an easy optimism, unburdened by the past or much of anything that might have been learned from it. This, too, is one of the ingredients in shaping an environment that puts history out of mind, at a disadvantage in shaping American character and culture, and in enabling the American people to take charge of their world.

It may have been comforting in the nineteenth century for Americans to believe that God protected them from foreign invasion, but what most clearly sustained American independence was British foreign policy, the British navy, the preoccupation of continental powers with national rivalries, and the then state of technology. History is not a substitute for prayer, but surely it is a reminder, as one historian has pointed out, that man should not "count on miracles."[2] History introduces a tragic sense where the innocent, the uninformed, would prefer not to be reminded of the ambiguities, incongruities, paradoxes, and complexities that inform our lives. History's job has been to remind us that indeed there was a serpent in Eden, but surely one purpose of the United States has been to deny it.

*H*istory is not "more or less bunk." It is a way of looking at things, a source of understanding, an important access to both self and society. If for many years Americans could choose to deny its relevance to their lives or impatiently disregard it, nonetheless the past is still there, still accessible, still in waiting, and a whole new set of circumstances suggest that there are new imperatives for establishing history firmly in the shared experience we call "common learning." The relentless course of equalitarianism in the United States has in recent years, at an accelerating pace, encouraged access to opportunities long denied to women, and to great numbers of blacks and other minorities. The pace and structure of urban life and industrial employment, in combination with the tentativeness of identity in an open society, have permeated our lives with loneliness. Man walks on the moon, satellites provide instant global communication, the world shrinks. Africa and Asia, once the target of Western missionaries, are emerging as great centers of power and promise in the contemporary world.

Somehow, in order to live in the world of dynamic change, we must take possession of it, not literally, not physically, but psychologically and philosophically. We must impose some kind of intellectual mastery in order to make life manageable and comprehensible. As the English historian E. H. Carr has pointed out, just as Europe is not a fact but a hypothesis that makes life intelligible, so history is not an accumulation of discrete facts, but a search for generalizations, a testing of hypotheses, an inquiry into the nature of causation in an effort to make human existence understandable.[3] We need to know how we got where we are in order to know where we are. We need to know where we are in order to deal effectively with the divisiveness, aspirations, tensions, and cross currents that are let loose by the events and movements that challenge and unsettle the comfortable certainties of time past. History allows man to understand his environment so that he may act upon it in a manner consistent with his knowledge and his sense of values. And, finally, the very equalitarian style that treats history as expendable creates conditions that make a sense of history essential to our psychological comfort.

History does not repeat itself, but the admonition that he who does not understand the past is condemned to repeat its mistakes constitutes one element in the case that can be made for historical study as an essential aspect of general learning. The astuteness with which Franklin Roosevelt and his advisers studied Woodrow Wilson's failure to enlist American support for the League of Nations is one reason that the United Nations was successfully launched upon a hopeful world in 1945.

Historical study, by incorporating the accident, paradox, mystery, and uncertainty into an understanding of causation, encourages a recognition of both the limits and the possibilities of human action. It promotes the wisdom that knows both what can be done and what cannot be done and is thus a powerful instrument for the application and conservation of intellectual energy.

A sense of the traditions and inheritance that shape our environment, an understanding of the conditions that have been delivered by the past to the present, necessarily inform the human intelligence as it takes the measures of the competing claims of inevitability and human initiative in human affairs. No one can study the presidential years of Abraham Lincoln without being impressed by how greatly he was both controlled by events and, in turn, controlled events, and how sensitively he understood the limits within which he was free to act if he would hold to his paramount purpose of saving the Union. Lincoln was possessed of a magnificent sense of history.

Now, a sense of history may lead to disenchantment. For it takes off the wraps, it tenderly removes illusions. To discover that Abraham Lincoln was the Great Emancipator less by choice than by necessity, reluctantly rather than purposefully, may remove some of the brightness from his halo, but it also strengthens our knowledge of the priorities, complexities, and uncertainties with which he dealt. We watch him acting in history, not in Heaven where we have assigned him, and thus learn something of the limits and the opportunities that shape our individual prospects.

If history is one of the ingredients that provide a kind of social glue, an adhesiveness that helps to keep us from flying apart into a mass of uncontrolled individual atoms, it is also the stuff that informs a sense of self, that clarifies our own particular histories, and that shapes the contemplation and self-discovery that underwrites individual identity. And while the admonition, "Know thyself," may at first appear to be self-centered, even narcissistic, hostile to social need and purpose, a brief moment of consideration will suggest that individuals secure in their own identities are a necessary support for a society secure in its own.

*T*o say all this, however, is not to say what must be in an educational experience that falls under the rubric, "Common Learning." It is seductively simple to think that it is possible to reach agreement on which key events, outstanding individuals, dynamic ideas, pervasive values; which achievements of the past, indeed which disasters, which riddles, which traditions most deserve inclusion in the educational experience of all people. There is something wonderfully appealing about the circumstances of not much more than a hundred years ago when President Eliot approached Henry Adams with a request that he join the Harvard faculty to teach history. As Adams tells it, "The two full Professors of History . . . could not cover the ground. Between Gurney's classical courses and Torrey's modern ones, lay a gap of a thousand years, which Adams was expected to fill."[4] Imagine! A three-man department to teach all the history there was. I do not exaggerate the confidence nor the naiveté of that earlier day. Listen to Lord Acton, preparing the prospectus for the multi-volume *Cambridge Modern History* of which he was to be the editor: ". . . Now that all information is within reach, and every problem has become capable of solution."[5] It is tempting to wish ourselves back in those self-confident times, but the temptation must be avoided. They were more certain, but we are wiser. We know that we must make choices, be selective, guard against our biases and assumptions, unleash and yet be wary of our imaginations and intuitions, and reach interpretations that will serve us as best they can as we clarify and comprehend our universe.

That is a large order. Fortunately, experience, history indeed, can give us some guidance in such matters, for there have been three notable models for incorporating history into a program in general learning. The first, developed at Columbia after World War I and echoed at Harvard after World War II, used history as an instrument for imparting right values. At Columbia, one purpose was the acculturation of an increasingly Jewish clientele, another was providing a corrective for radical understandings of the past. At Harvard, a more general concern over the technological thrust of American society and fear of an improperly and inadequately trained democracy led to the prescription of history as a social bonding agent. The Columbia-Harvard model, as Professor David Potts has pointed out, used different materials — Columbia, its Western Civilization course; Harvard, a cluster of history-dominated electives—to advance the purpose of value indoctrination.

Another model, developed at the University of Chicago in the 1930s and elaborated on at Union College in the 1970s, is essentially more cerebral, less concerned with value formation than with modes of thought and inquiry that inform the development of what might be defined as an intellectual style. In this model, history joins the social sciences in providing perspectives in comparative culture, insights into the role of institutions in human behavior, and similar experiences in the application of reason to enduring human questions and problems.

The third model is in the process of development at Harvard under the leadership of Dean Henry Rosovsky. For, while much about the Harvard reforms has been blown beyond understanding by the press, Harvard's definition of history as one of five major approaches to knowledge gives history a justification beyond the concern with values or social science that shaped the earlier models. In the current Harvard model, values and the linkage with social science are not necessarily absent, but neither are they determining. Harvard does not propose with its history requirement to graduate either better men and women or brighter men and women, but it does expect to prepare a generation of graduates who can read a newspaper with greater understanding and with a greater sense of the complexity of the events that have shaped man's past.

At a session of the American Historical Association's annual meetings in San Francisco in 1978 a group of historians addressed the question: "Is History an essential part of programs for general education?" As Professor Potts, author of the principal paper on that occasion, pointed out, general education has interested historians less as an historical or educational question than as a matter of campus politics and course enrollments, but he also suggested that "the plight of history as an academic discipline" might now direct practitioners of history to a serious consideration of the relationships of history, the liberal arts, and higher education at a time when all three are beleaguered. Furthermore, he suggested that there exists an opportunity to link Harvard's use of history as an approach to knowledge with the concern of earlier models with values and rational social science. Because the historical method is both more and less than scientific, possessing a point-of-view, necessarily leaping from the known to the unknown, from what was to what must have been, it relies on intuition, imagination, the mystery of what it means to be human. It, in the words of Douglas Sloan of Columbia, recognizes the emotions, the will, and intuition, bringing together "scientific insight, artistic insight, and moral insight."[6] In effect, as Professor Potts ably argued, "history is well-suited as a discipline to help restore . . . [a] balanced humanistic perspective through programs of general education."[7]

How that balanced perspective is to be reclaimed is beyond our immediate responsibility, but it is obvious that the task belongs to the schools as well as to the colleges and universities, and that in the absence of any great sense of urgency among the professors it will require extraordinary, exhausting, courageous leadership from academic administrators. I do not doubt that a humanistic reclamation movement is already under way, but I do believe that it would be a mistake to assume that there is only one way or only a half dozen ways to resocialize and rehumanize the American college graduate. In recognizing our ailment, however, surely we are well on our way to discovering the cures.

NOTES

1. Samuels, Ernest (Ed.) *The Education of Henry Adams* (Boston, Houghton Mifflin, 1974) p. 498.

2. As quoted in Carr, Edward Hallett. *What is History?* (New York, Alfred A. Knopf, 1962) p. 36.

3. *Ibid.,* p. 76.

4. *The Education of Henry Adams,* p. 300.

5. As quoted in Carr. *What is History?* p. 3.

6. Sloan, Douglas. "On the Possibilities of Newness," *Teachers College Record,* vol. 79 (February 1978), pp. 329-338.

7. Potts, David B. "Is History an Essential Part of Programs for General Education? Answers Past and Present," pp. 3-4. Xerox copy of a paper delivered at the annual meeting of the American Historical Association, San Francisco, December 28, 1978.

Contemporary
Organizations

BY ROSABETH MOSS KANTER

CHAPTER FOUR

$\mathcal{M}$uch of the rhetoric used by advocates of more general education for citizens is echoed by proponents of an education designed to produce generally informed managers in our business organizations. Indeed, a recent prize-winning essay in the *Harvard Business Review* placed much of the responsibility for America's decaying productivity on the many narrowly trained experts serving as corporate chief executives. If the need for generalist perspectives is as widespread and serious as that indictment suggests, we might well wonder why those who advance the case for less specialized preparation of citizens, and, particularly, of business managers, fail so signally to have impact.

A significant part of the answer lies in the reward systems institutionalized in both American society and in our organizations. To an astonishing degree, they all reward narrow rather than broad perspectives. In business organizations the push toward specialization starts at the entry level. Candidates are selected more for special skills than for general capacity. The MBA degree is currently highly desired by students as well as employers; specialized MBAs are sought as if the ordinary

MBA were not already specialized enough. Performance measures for employees are primarily short-term, favoring those who can readily attack closely defined problems without necessary reference to the fate of the whole organization.

In most organizations, much of the real power is held by functions rather than individuals, and most formal promotion mechanisms reinforce functional specialization. For the organization, the reason is simple: why train people for work about which they lack knowledge when already-trained people exist? After all, every corporate "investment" needs to generate an appropriate "return." Such is the message of human capital theory. The consequence is that when organizations look for truly *general* managers, there are none to be found. The nearest equivalent, it appears, is an executive acquired from another organization.

Similar pressures for specialization are found in the elaboration of the idea of the professional, a description once reserved for those engaged in a very few special fields—medicine, law, architecture—and now used by nearly everyone. The word has now become little more than a label that conveys a sense of status and privilege to any sort of work and any sort of worker. Even within the professions, further specialization counts significantly. Medical specialists earn more than generalists. In fact, until recently, generalists were not even accepted as associates for any hospital in the City of Boston, which, by most standards, is the premier medical science and training center in the world.

These tendencies to specialize become still greater when, as now, the economy is weak. All the advantages in job markets, both outside and inside organizations, accrue to specialists and "professionals." Anyone unfortunate enough to be a generalist is encouraged to retrain. For example, Ph.D.s in comparative literature or language are returning to school for MBAs. Actually since the value of a college or liberal arts education is also dropping as it becomes less distinguishing and, probably, less substantive as well, it is not even *possible* to gain nonspecialist advanced degrees. What study is available for one who wants a doctorate in broad knowledge and perspective, and an increased capacity to recognize patterns and useful links among disparate areas? If we really want to promote the idea of "general" education, we need to make real opportunities and reinforcing rewards available. Rhetoric must be matched by institutional and organizational realities.

Despite the absence of mechanisms encouraging common learning across fields, the need for them is as great as ever — perhaps greater yet. To understand and manage contemporary organizations or societies whose institutions are largely rooted in such organizations, one must be able to see beyond individuals or discrete acts.

In the study of organizations and institutions, there is a shift away from the assumptions of individualism, which I have labeled elsewhere as the *voluntaristic* model. The voluntaristic model includes these assumptions:

1. Organizations and individuals can operate as closed systems, controlling whatever is needed for their operation. They can be understood on their own terms, according to their internal dynamics, without much reference to factors in their environment, their location in a larger social structure, or their links to other organizations or individuals.
2. Such social actors, whether collective or individual, have relatively free choice, limited only by their own abilities. But since there is also consensus about *how* and toward what ends social actors should operate, there is clarity and singularity of purpose.
3. The individual is the ultimate unit and the ultimate actor. Problems

in social life therefore stem from individual characteristics of three kinds: failures of will, or inadequate motivation; incompetence, or differences in talent; and greed, or the willful pursuit of self-interest. There is little need to look beyond individual characteristics, abilities, or motives to understand why the coordinated social activities we call institutional patterns do not always produce social goods.

4. Differentiation of the activities of social actors is not only possible but necessary, and coordination will largely take care of itself. Specialization is desirable, both for individuals and organizations, and neither should be asked to go beyond their primary purposes. (Thus, in Milton Friedman's terms, corporations should pursue only profits and forget about social responsibilities.) As a corollary, it is not necessary for specialized individuals or organizations to know much about the acts of others in different areas. Coordination is itself a specialty, and the coordinators (whether they be markets, managers, or integrating disciplines) will ensure that activities fit together in a coherent and beneficial way.

Of course, many of these assumptions have been under revision or attack for many years. The notion of the corporation as an individual actor writ large once informed much legal thought, but recently, there has been increasing acknowledgement that such social organizations are too complex to make the analogy to an individual appropriate. Beginning in the 1960s the academic study of organizations, as well as managerial practice, moved away from closed-system assumptions, especially as it became increasingly clear that organizations are highly dependent upon and sometimes shaped by turbulent and uncertain environments. Tracing social problems back to individual characteristics has similarly been challenged, and neither "blame the victim" nor "blame the leader" arguments have been nearly as prominent in American social thought over the last few decades as previously. Consensus about the proper conduct of social actors and the proper ends of institutions, if it ever existed, has been undermined by events. It is no longer possible to talk about *the* American family or *the* American community, for example, as though there were only one type rather than a diverse and pluralistic group. In today's view, organizational goals are not "natural" and "given" but the result of an organization's "dominant coalition" formed by a bargaining process that favors some interests over others.

Voluntaristic models themselves arise under certain predictable social circumstances. These situations include economic expansion, where opportunity and power seem limitless, and where it thus appears that only individual limitations can prevent success. They include circumstances in which one's own social group is dominant over forces in the environment, and is able to control its activities by predicting and therefore mastering all of the elements needed to operate. Furthermore, in such times, opposing forces or groups are unorganized, unactivated, or quiescent. The environment is stable rather than turbulent, permitting the illusion that differences in the effectiveness of individuals or organizations is based largely on the quality of their own decisions. This is an illusion because under these circumstances it is difficult to see the conditions in the environment that make such success possible; they are so predictable and so taken for granted that they retreat into the background. Consensus appears natural because clear challenging groups have not arisen.

Most of these conditions no longer apply to American society. Despite periodic longings for the establishment of simple and bounded "perfect communities," that could wall themselves off from the outside and operate consensually but mechanically, Americans must reconcile themselves to a world that is contradictory and puzzling rather than orderly and con-

trolled. No single social group or set of organizations domi-
nates, and America no longer controls those who supply the
resources it needs to carry out its activities. Even the best leader
may not be able to control an organization, or accomplish all of
its objectives, in a turbulent environment in which the organization's success may depend less on its *own* decisions than on
decisions made elsewhere and by others.

Knowledge of resource limits and a seemingly unmanage-
able economy have, however, brought back another kind of
voluntaristic or individualistic thinking, another predictable response to such circumstances. Groups at the top of the hierarchy
favor individualism as a way to consolidate their positions and
reduce competition. If individuals are assumed to get what they
deserve, independently from larger patterns and larger forces in
social life, then those at the top can keep what they have.

It is doubtful, however, that this kind of self-interest-based
individualism can prevail against the increasing awareness of
institutional and organizational interdependence in a complex
and turbulent world. In many companies, corporate leaders
increasingly recognize the need to move beyond the assumption
that success is due to individual deal-making and toward the
management and manipulation of the system in its environ-
mental context.

To demonstrate the need to focus on, and learn about, the
interconnections between areas of knowledge that bear on social
institutions, look at two phenomena that challenge individualistic or voluntaristic assumptions: first, the patterned nature of
organizational life—the shaping of seemingly individual acts by
location of individuals in that pattern; and second, the
recalcitrance of institutions — the inability to guarantee that
organizations do just what they are designed to do, or that they
will change when asked.

*T*o say that individual acts are shaped or patterned by location in a social structure is not to deny the active role of human beings in constructing or shaping their response to circumstances. However, it does indicate that people are limited by their tools; they respond not to an endless array of possibilities but rather to the choices at hand. In essence, this perspective also holds that individual motives or seemingly individually based problems cannot be understood apart from social circumstances and the interconnections between different parts of the system.

For example, family life is supposedly the bastion of individualism since it is the individual's retreat from public life. Yet, as many recent authors have pointed out, family life is shaped and patterned by its connections to the economic system. The decisions, strategies, and activities of economic organizations affect the nature of family life, through variables that link both systems: time and scheduling, rewards and resources, occupational cultures, and the emotional climate at work.

The amount of time demanded by occupations and the timing of occupational events in organizations are among the most obvious and important ways these systems interact. Family events and routines are usually built around work rhythms, and much of the timing of events in the society as a whole is predicated on assumptions about the hours, days, and months people are most likely to be working or not working — the allocation of their energy across time and social space. The income generated by membership in economic organizations not only determines life-style and consumption level in rather predictable ways, but also helps to determine the relative resources over which each family member has initial control. Power and dominance in families is thus shaped by the memberships that individuals in those families have in other organizations and the resources they can bring into their families. Furthermore, roles in these extra-family organizations, and especially in economic organizations, provide a culture or a world view that affects the decisions people make in their families. Marriage trends, child rearing practices, and family values all vary across families with members' occupational and economic memberships. And finally, people's emotional states directly carry responses to one institution to another. Unpleasant, frustrating jobs are related to family tension.

Location inside organizations also affects individual behaviors and motivations. People in situations with great opportunity for future progress exhibit patterns very different from those in low-opportunity situations: they have higher aspirations, greater self-confidence and self-esteem, greater attachment to work, lower rates of turnover and disengagement, more task-oriented relationships, an active sense that they are in charge of events rather than controlled by them, a disposition to prepare for the future more consistently, and a positive feeling about their ability. Location in positions of advantage — positions with mobility prospects, jobs that can be enlarged, and chances for greater future gains—or disadvantage, seems to be a more potent explanation for the lesser economic success of women or members of minority groups than individual characteristics. To the extent that selection and tracking systems exist not only in employing organizations but also in organizations preparing people for jobs, the patterned assignment of women and minorities to low-opportunity situations determines much of the resulting behavior and motivation.

Many other aspects of organizational behavior have been reanalyzed in similar ways. For example, certain well-known bureaucratic pathologies, such as leadership styles characterized by control, overly close supervision, rules mindedness, and territorial defensiveness are associated with organizational situations rather than individual characteristics. Relative power or powerlessness is the issue. When people lack the resources needed to do their job, and when their outward influence is limited, they feel powerless and tend to turn to control over others in their own limited domain and to use whatever weapons they do possess to assert at least minimal control.

Thus, informed citizens need to learn the limits imposed on their own and other's actions by the design of organizations and by institutional interdependencies. This learning also encourages empathy — If I were located where you are, I might feel the same way. It encourages attention to the underlying sources of problem behavior, rather than to punishment of the individual. It encourages humility: the knowledge that beneficial circumstances and not just individual superiority may be responsible for success. And, paradoxically, it is also freeing. Recognition of the socially patterned nature of conduct permits the person to step aside, review his or her actions, and, by noting the effect of external forces, gain some mastery of them. Understanding these larger patterns permits the broader society to remove constraints or add options to encourage constructive behavior. But change leads to another topic.

*I*ndividualistic thinking often attributes the recalcitrance of institutions—their failings, their ill effects, their lack of responsiveness to changing circumstances or demands — to the motives or incompetences of individuals. But much of this recalcitrance comes from the paradoxical nature of organizations themselves. They do not do what they are designed to do; they do not provide benefits without incurring costs; they do not solve one set of problems without creating others; and they are difficult to change. Interventions in institutional life themselves create unanticipated consequences. Of course many organizations run smoothly, carry out their purposes effectively, and provide a surplus of benefits over costs. But it is important to know how successful organizations differ from those that fail, to know why the plans of certain organizations do not always work out as expected, or why organizations cannot shift course easily.

One set of explanations is that organizations have multiple and often conflicting goals. Official goals and operative goals are very different. Even associations formed for very limited purposes may take on other purposes as they acquire members. There is also no guarantee of identity of interest among the groups with a stake in an organization's operation. It is even difficult to know when an organization has accomplished the purpose for which it was designed because it may have so many purposes for so many people.

The fact that organizations cannot be rationally designed and controlled is illustrated by the substantial literature on bureaucracy and its discontents. For years after Max Weber's model of bureaucracy was translated into English, critics argued that human nature made it impossible ever to attain Weber's ideal type. But close examination reveals it is the very *success* of bureaucratic mechanisms that leads to many of the phenomena that undermine bureaucracy.

For example, bureaucracy is based on delegation and differentiation. But the more extensively an organization differentiates, the more likely tensions will arise between subgroups pursuing their limited ends rather than the goals of the whole — a phenomenon called "suboptimization." Bureaucracy also requires specialization, but the more the organization develops and relies on specialists, the more likely it is to create what Veblen called "trained incapacity," the inability for specialists to manage any task outside of their own domain. The better they get at their specialized ability, then perhaps the less their ability to learn anything else requiring a different style of thought. Further, bureaucracy is based on calculable rules that specify in advance the elements that enter into performance. To the extent that people rely on the rules in lieu of judgment, they are likely to suffer rigidity in the face of change. Yet change is necessary, since not all situations can be specified in advance. Impersonal and measurable performance criteria, another characteristic of bureaucratic organizations, tend to produce another unintended consequence: participants can gear their performance to only the minimal acceptable standard, subverting the formal objectives.

Other elements of bureaucratic organizations have the same paradoxical results. First, clear lines of authority can result in an abdication of responsibility at lower levels. Second, graded careers in distinct hierarchies can lead to rigidity in the deployment of people. Third, segmental participation conflicts with the human tendency to be a "whole person" and to invest an organizational role with more individual identity than the role requires.

Organizations reflect agreements on the part of many different people, with many different aims and purposes, and often from many different social worlds, to cooperate for the purpose of attaining a rather specific shared objective. The manifest difficulty of attempting to erect narrow boundaries around one slice of human existence and to suspend all other activities, interests, and behavioral tendencies, should not surprise us. Indeed, it is somewhat surprising that there should be any coordinated, cooperative effort in organizations, and among organizations in a society, especially in a pluralistic society marked by an emphasis on individualism. What is remarkable is not whether the thing is done well, but whether it is done at all.

There are numerous examples of the extent to which attempts to control behavior in organizations, or the behavior of organizations, leads to unintended, if not negative, consequences. To produce quality education, reading test scores of schools across school systems are compared. All activity in the classroom is then geared toward improving test scores, and the children learn no other subjects. In an attempt to reward police officers fairly and promote them on the basis of productivity, quantitative measurements of performance, such as the number of arrests, are imposed. Suddenly, arrest rates go up with no change in criminal behavior. Of course, the substitution of a single purpose or measure for the larger values or purposes of the organization is rather benign compared to some other unintended consequences, such as pollution, poor employee health, or changed family patterns. In the latter case, one organization—the federal government— has created serious unintended consequences by intervening into the lives of those in other institutions. For example, in order to help children who were not in a stable family, aid to dependent children was made contingent on the single status of parents. As it turned out, this created a disincentive to marry.

Christopher Stone, lawyer, and author of *Where the Law Ends,* [1] in his examination of the lack of impact of most legal sanctions against corporations in shaping socially responsible behavior, makes clear that the recalcitrance of organizations is not a matter of individual will or motivation. It cannot be resolved by imposing stiffer fines or by introducing ethics courses in business schools. Because of the very complexity, internal differentiation, size, and multiple purposes of complex organizations, sanctions based on individualistic assumptions will not work. Executives would prefer not to go to jail, but applying such individual sanctions requires that it be possible to single out accountable individuals.

There are many arguments against imposing such sanctions. First, individuals are dispensable in large-scale organizations; an organization can usually replace executives more easily than it can change direction. The law is only one force operating on conduct; other forces stem from career pressures and reward structures. Assigning the responsibility for appropriate action to individuals, even at the top, ignores organizational communication processes that often screen the top from knowledge or information of operations at lower levels. However, lower level individuals often are not worth suing or punishing. Most important, problems often are caused not by acts of individuals, but by the cumulative and interactive results of many different acts or functions, each of which contributes only a piece of the problem.

The solution is not to treat an organization like an individual, holding over it the threat of later sanctions, but rather to understand and intervene directly in the decision processes of the organization in its ongoing operations. Insuring that organizations conform to societal purposes requires that the desired perspectives are implanted in the core decision processes of the organization. It requires becoming involved with the formulation of the patterns themselves, rather than holding accountable individuals whose acts have largely been shaped by those patterns. The web of activities comprising institutions — their social structures — are beyond either the view or the grasp of any individual.

The difficulty of guaranteeing that organizations do only what was intended, no more and no less, is in part a function of the numerous overt or hidden institutional patterns that permit particular forms of organized cooperative activity. Social scientists are currently debating the extent of the articulation among all of the institutions of a society. But whether or not one subscribes to the notion of a unified and integrated social system, the ability of organizations to operate in particular ways depends on a variety of seemingly unrelated decisions made in other institutions that determine the forms of behavior that are appropriate.

Some have argued that, in our society, families, schools, and other related institutions are designed to meet the needs of employing organizations, although they may also limit the extent to which economic organizations can require particular kinds of behavior from their members. History and culture, as carried by those institutions that socialize the young, affect the shape of economic and political organizations. We see this by noting the unique configurations in Japanese companies as compared to American ones — the stress on loyalty, teamwork, commitment to the company rather than to a job, widespread "lifetime" employment, acceptance of authority, concern with maintaining status gradations, and the like. We also see it in the historical forces that helped shape the premier American corporations as social institutions. In the formative years of the large industrial corporation, 1890-1910, the labor pool included a large proportion of relatively unskilled migrants from other countries or rural areas who were unaccustomed to the discipline of industrial work and maintained an attachment to places of origin. Turnover and labor conflict were both extensive. Jobs and job hierarchies were designed with these conditions in sight, thus giving rise to the fragmentation and simplification of tasks and long, graded job ladders. Some analysts have argued, however, that schools soon took on the role of industrial trainers; more universal public education filled the needs of employers for work-habituated employees. Indeed, in a study of a nursery school in Ann Arbor, Michigan, I once noted that the school was training three- and four-year-olds to be comfortable in bureaucratic organizations, dubbing the product the "organization child."

Thus, some of the seeming recalcitrance of organizations comes from the numerous other social institutions with which they are intertwined. They are bound by decisions, sometimes coordinated and coherent, sometimes idiosyncratic and scattered, made in many other places. They are similarly bound by their own histories. Once an organizational pattern is established, it is difficult to change. Again, the explanations lie not so much in human nature as in the nature of organized social life. Individuals are not naturally conservative, although people do prefer the known to the unknown. But social life forces an interest in stable patterns. Cooperative activity itself is not possible unless people can count on the stability of structures and behavioral patterns. Indeed, we rely extensively on such patterns without even being aware of it. These unquestioned expectations permit us to function without renegotiating every bit of activity that takes place, and it is only because others can be expected to fully honor these commitments that a complex society can do its work.

Change therefore requires, as a first step, the unraveling of a network of expectations. Only then is it possible to learn new patterns that form around the particular activity in question. Even though, in a certain sense, change is ubiquitous in our society, it is also strongly resisted because it disrupts patterns and expectations, and because some people who benefit from the status quo may lose ground under different conditions. An organization's history can be seen in just this light, as the build-up of a network of expectations incorporated in structures and patterns that permit people to function rather automatically.

My own current studies of transformations in American corporations show how understandable it is that the most "progressive" companies often are also the newest and thus least bound by their own histories (with the exception of a few that designed themselves to be progressive and innovative from the beginning). Change in older, established industries is so difficult that it may take decades to accomplish. (Of course, change or institutional recalcitrance also can derive from individual greed — motivation based on current benefits — or from the obvious difference in how constituent groups view the desirability of change.)

The last paradoxical characteristic of organizations is that solutions themselves give rise to new problems. Benefits do not come without cost, and those elements or interests that are suppressed in the service of meeting one limited purpose will often emerge later; it is impossible to limit the breadth of human interests too stringently. Failure to solve problems does mean dropping out of the game, but successes themselves generate "upside" risks. For example, companies that do well face the very difficult problems of managing growth. They have to add and train people quickly without losing their coherence. They may have to commit many scarce resources to one area to honor the commitments that their growth entails. And "success" may even undermine the atmosphere of challenge and sacrifice that helped an organization develop and grow. Utopian communities often lose the devotion of their members as they become affluent because initial commitment was based, in part, on shared struggle and the collective excitement it brings.

$\mathcal{I}$t *is* possible to manage organizations effectively, but this requires balance: for example, balance between enough stable patterns to function and adequate flexibility in the face of change. One necessary ingredient of the leadership of America's "society of organizations" is enlightenment—conscious awareness of the paradoxical and patterned nature of organizational life, the interconnectedness of decisions at many levels and among many organizations and institutions. It means seeing beyond individualism, in a number of senses: seeing beyond individual motives and into the difficulties and complexities of cooperative activity, and seeing beyond the proximate causes of individual decisions into the web of institutional relations that make such individual decisions seem the only reasonable outcome.

To survive in our complex world society, and to steer an intelligent course via organizations established to serve human ends, requires "common learning"—the ability to see patterns, the ability to understand interconnections and interdependencies, the ability to place individual acts in context, and the ability to tolerate the ultimately uncontrollable and fragile nature of cooperative activity and our vulnerability in the face of that fragility.

One simple answer to the question of "Why encourage broad learning in the social sciences?" is found in Murphy's

Law: Things never work as planned. The more variables that we can take into account, then the more can a larger number of problems be understood, and, ultimately, the more activities can be designed to work, at least approximately, the way the designers of those activities—we, the citizens and leaders—intended.

NOTE

1. Stone, Christopher. *Where the Law Ends: Social Control of Corporate Behavior* (New York, Harper & Row, 1976).

.

The Natural World

BY LEWIS THOMAS, M.D.

CHAPTER FIVE

*A*lthough science depends upon surprise, only succeeds when it achieves surprise, and lives off surprise, there is something intolerable to the scientists themselves about sustained, enduring surprise. It is necessary to explain the thing, whatever, away as quickly and flatly as possible, and whenever possible in mathematical terms.

The teaching of science suffers because of this.

You would expect the physicists and astronomers to spend their lives goggle-eyed, giggling in public, exploding from time to time into long peals of laughter at the oddity of the things they catch glimpses of in nature. The biologists are so frequently flabbergasted these days by the everyday events in their laboratories that they should be laughing and crying at the same time over their instruments. But it is not so. Out come the papers, one astonishment after another, written in language as cleansed of ambiguity as language can be, as lean and sparing as strings of words can be made, never hinting at surprise, always laying out the facts and the best — and as well the several alternative second-best — explanations of the facts, as though the findings had been the most natural and expected of things. The new facts can usually be made to fit with at least some of the facts at hand, and are. Order in the universe at large is preserved, along with order at the innermost, benthic depths of living cells and the infinitely small working parts of the atom, no matter how many firmly embedded ideas about how the place works are destroyed by the new bits of information brought in by science. It is a coherent world; we know this in our bones even though we continue to find in it a complexity beyond our comprehension. It fits and holds together; this is the central dogma, and every new scientific observation contributes sooner or later to the stability and imperturbability of this underlying truth. The ways in which it works, the details, are always a surprise but only transiently: at bottom is the solid idea of order and coordination, taken for granted, assumed.

There are two ways to learn about science. One, the method used in most of the courses taught in college, is to look at the entire structure as it stands today, all fitted neatly together fact by fact, detail by detail; learn all of the participants by name and number, see how they fit together, and your mind is home and dry, in command of science. The second way, which I am only guessing at because of never having seen it tried, is to concentrate attention on the weak spots, the things under the rug, the almost tidy but still intrinsically and unfixably *untidiable* parts, the unstable, soon-to-be-replaced aspects. In short, the areas of ignorance and the places to station oneself in anticipation of revolution and revelation, the best seats for the parade on its way up the avenue with the band playing not Sousa but the Art of Fugue, one surprise after another.

Scientists like to teach the facts as they firmly stand, tending to shy away from matters where the available facts make up only a smattering, even more from problems containing conflicting facts, ambiguities and paradoxes. They have a deep fear of confusing their students, and a latent fear of confusing themselves. Because the body of scientific knowledge is, by the very nature of the enterprise, made up of great masses of reductionist detail, and the masses of detail tend to double every few years, the teachers of science feel it a hard enough task to present what they can of the detail without having to cope at the same time with speculative aspects of the field.

It is at least partly because of this that some of the brightest and most talented of students are turned away from a deep interest in science in their undergraduate college years. They are misled by their classroom experiences into the view that science is nothing but a massive aggregation of small details, none of them especially interesting in themselves. Worse, they gain the impression that almost everything that can be learned is already known; there are satisfactory explanations at hand for almost all phenomena in nature; all that is needed is to surround and digest all the facts and soon, with a few odd details and anomalies here and there waiting to be tidied up, the task of science will be completed. There are better things to do with a life than to enter a line of work so near its own completion, and so the students look elsewhere, except for the minority who are able to perceive the real profundity of human ignorance about nature, and the majority of premedical students who diligently and aggressively study science not for its own sake, not at all for the fun of it, but as a necessary and painful rite of passage on the way to becoming doctors.

Indeed, the premedical students are themselves a large part of the difficulty in the teaching of science. They believe — and because of their great numbers the college faculties tend to concur — that there is a special and specific body of scientific knowledge in biology, chemistry, and physics which they must master if they are to be eligible for medical school admission, and the curriculum is automatically altered and doctored to meet this need. There are separate, segregated courses in physics and chemistry on many campuses that are labelled in the catalogue as "premedical," and all sorts of offerings in biological science are put together because of a presumed or hoped-for relevance to medicine. It is no fun being a premedical student these days because of the intensity of the competition. The students believe with justification that they can only become acceptable by achieving straight A's in as many science courses as possible, and, as a corollary, by avoiding any nonscience courses in which there is a risk of not being graded A. They know, from their own reliable sources of gossip, that the medical school admissions committees will place their application folders in different stacks depending on their numerical class standing, and they are off and running in the competition from the first day of the freshman year. Indeed, most of them began the combat toward medical school in high school, some even in grammar school, and they live in the belief that if they fail to get the topmost grades their lives will be destroyed. It is hard to teach science, harder still to learn *about* science, in such company, with all the fun taken out of it.

The medical school deans could do a lot to improve college science if they had a real mind to do so. They could, for instance, stipulate that there is a genuine minimum requirement for premedical science, and while no student should be penalized for exceeding this minimum out of intellectual interest, no student will necessarily be benefitted by doing so. Another thing that I wish the deans would do, although I know as a former dean they can't and won't, but I wish it anyway: they should let it be known that henceforth a fixed proportion of each entering class in their medical schools will be recruited from students who rank in the *middle* of the class. I confess to some apprehension for the future of my profession if its practitioners are exclusively made up of the top 5 percent grade-achievers and examination-takers. I also wish they would abandon, once and for all, the MCAT examinations, or at least give up looking at the scores. But I digress.

The greatest of all the accomplishments in twentieth-century science has been the discovery of human ignorance. We live, as never before, in puzzlement about nature, the universe, and ourselves most of all. It is a new experience for the species. A century ago, after the turbulence caused by Darwin and Wallace had subsided and the central idea of natural selection had been grasped and accepted, we thought we knew everything essential about evolution. In the eighteenth century there were no huge puzzles; human reason was all you needed for figuring out the universe. And for most of the earlier centuries, the Church provided both the questions and the answers, neatly packaged. Now, for the first time in human history, we are catching glimpses of our incomprehension. We can still make up stories to explain the world as we always have, but now the stories have to be confirmed by experiment and then, once confirmed, reconfirmed. This is the scientific method, and having started on this line there can be no turning back. We are obliged to grow up in skepticism, requiring proofs for every assertion about nature, and there is no way out except to move ahead and plug away, hoping for comprehension in the future but living in a condition of intellectual instability for the long time being.

It is the puzzles that lead to progress, not so much because the solving of a particular puzzle leads directly to a new piece of understanding, but because the puzzle leads to *work*. There is a phenomenon in entomology known as stigmergy, a term invented by Grassé meaning "to incite to work." When three or four termites are collected together in a chamber they wander about aimlessly, getting nothing in particular done, but when more termites are added the situation changes and they begin to build. It is the presence of other termites, in sufficient numbers at close quarters, that produces the work: they pick up each other's fecal pellets, stack them up in neat columns, and then, when the columns are precisely the right height they reach across and turn the perfect arches which form the foundation of the termitarium. No single termite knows how to do any of this, but as soon as there are enough of them gathered together, they become, collectively, flawless architects, sensing their distances from each other although blind, building an immensely complicated structure with its own air conditioning and humidity control.

Very little is understood about this kind of collective behavior. It is out of fashion these days to talk of "super-organisms," as Wheeler once talked, but there simply are not enough reductionist details in hand to allow the phenomenon of termites and other social insects to be explained away. Some very good guesses can be made about their chemical signalling systems, but the plain fact that they exhibit something like a collective intelligence by simply being in touch with each other is a mystery, or anyway an unsolved problem, perhaps containing important implications for social life in general.

This is the best example I could think of for an introduction to biological science in college. It should be taught for its strangeness, and for the ambiguity of its meaning. It should be taught to premedical students, who need lessons early on in their careers about the uncertainties in science.

College students, and for that matter high school students, should be exposed very early, perhaps at the very outset, to the big arguments currently going on among the scientists. This is the best way I can imagine to stimulate their interest, and, with luck, engage their absorbed attention. Few things in life are as absorbing to watch as a good fight between highly trained and skilled adversaries. But the young students are told very little about the major disagreements of the day; they may be taught something about the arguments between Darwinians and their opponents a century ago, long since settled, but they do not realize that similar disputes about other matters, many of them touching profound issues for our understanding of nature, are still going on and, indeed, comprise an essential feature of the scientific process. There is, I fear, a reluctance on the part of science teachers to talk about such things, based on the belief that before students can appreciate what the arguments are about they must learn and master the details, the "fundamentals." I would be willing to see some experiments along this line, and I have in mind several examples of contemporary doctrinal dispute in which the drift of the argument can be readily perceived without the requirement of deep or elaborate knowledge of the subject.

There is, for one, the problem of animal awareness. One school of investigators, devoted to the study of animal behavior, has it that human beings are unique in the possession of consciousness, differing from all other creatures in being able to think things over, capitalize on past experience, and hazard informed guesses at the future. Other animals, "lower" (with possible exceptions made for chimpanzees, whales, and dolphins), cannot do such things with their minds; they live from moment to moment with brains that are programed to respond to contingencies in the environment automatically or by conditioning. The behaviorists, in fact, believe that this accounts for human mental activity as well, although they dislike that word "mental." On the other side are some ethologists who seem to me more generous-minded, like Donald Griffin, who see no compelling reasons to doubt that animals in general are quite capable of real thinking and do quite a lot of it, not as densely as human thinking because of the lack of language and the resultant lack of metaphors to help the thought along, but thinking nonetheless.

The point about this argument is not that one side or the other is in possession of a more powerful array of convincing facts, quite the opposite. There are not enough facts to sustain a genuine debate of any length; the question of animal awareness is an unsettled one. In the circumstance, I am permitted to put forward the following notion about a small beetle, the mimosa girdler, which undertakes three pieces of linked, sequential behavior: 1) finding a mimosa tree and climbing up the trunk and out to the end of a branch, 2) cutting a longitudinal slit and laying within it five or six eggs, and 3) crawling back on the limb and girdling it neatly down to the cambium (an 8 to 10 hour task of hard labor from which the beetle gains no food for itself, only the certainty that the branch will promptly die and fall to the ground in the next brisk wind, and the larvae thus enabled to hatch and grow in an abundance of dead wood). I propose, in total confidence that even though I am probably wrong nobody today can prove that I am wrong, that the beetle is not doing these three things out of blind instinct, like a little machine, but is thinking its way along, just as we would think. The difference is that we possess enormous brains, crowded all the time with an infinite number of long thoughts, while the beetle's brain is only a few strings of neurones connected together in a modest network, capable therefore of only three *tiny* thoughts, coming into consciousness one after the other: find the right tree, get up there and lay eggs in a slit, then back up and spend the day killing the branch so the eggs can hatch; end of message. I would not go so far as to try anthropomorphizing the mimosa tree, for I really do not believe plants have minds at all, but something has to be said about the tree's role in this arrangement as a beneficiary; mimosas grow for 25 to 30 years and then die, unless they are vigorously pruned annually, in which case they can live to be a hundred. The beetle is a piece of good luck for the tree, but nothing more: an example, if you are collecting such examples, of pure chance working at its best in nature, what you might even wish to call good nature.

This brings me, by chance, to the second example of unsettlement in biology, currently being rather delicately discussed but not yet really argued over, for there is still only one orthodoxy and almost no opposition. This is the matter of chance itself, and the role played by blind chance in the arrangement of living things on the planet. It is, in the orthodox view, pure luck that evolution brought us to our present condition, and it might just as well have turned out any number of other, different ways, and might go in any unpredictable way for the future. There is, of course, nothing chancy about natural selection itself: it is an inevitable and solid fact that selection will always favor the advantaged individuals whose genes succeed best in propagating themselves within a changing environment. But the creatures acted upon by natural selection are themselves there to begin with as the result of chance: mutations (probably of much more importance during the long period of prokaryotic microbial life starting nearly 4 billion years ago), the endless sorting and resorting of genes within chromosomes during replication, perhaps recombination of genes across species lines at one time or another, and almost certainly the carrying of genes by viruses from one creature to another.

The argument comes when you contemplate the whole biosphere, the conjoined life of the earth. How could it have turned out to possess such stability and coherence, resembling as it does a system, a sort of enormous developing embryo, with nothing but chance events to determine its emergence? Lovelock and Margulis, facing this problem, have proposed the Gaia Hypothesis which proposes in brief that the earth is itself a form of life, "a complex entity involving the Earth's biosphere, atmosphere, oceans and soil; the totality constituting a feedback or cybernetic system which seeks an optional physical and chemical environment for life on this planet." Lovelock postulates, in addition, that "the physical and chemical condition of the surface of the Earth, of the atmosphere, and of the oceans has been and is actively made fit and comfortable by the presence of life itself."[1]

This notion is beginning to stir up a few signs of storm, and if it catches on, as I think it will, we will soon find the biological community split into fuming factions, one side saying that the evolved biosphere displays evidences of design and purpose, the other decrying such heresy, and I believe the students should learn as much as they can about the argument. W. F. Doolittle has recently attacked the Gaia Hypothesis in an essay in *CoEvolution Quarterly*[2], asking among other things " . . . how does Gaia know if she is too cold or too hot, and how does she instruct the biosphere to behave accordingly?" This is not a deadly criticism in a world where we do not actually understand, in anything like real detail, how even Dr. Doolittle manages the stability and control of his own internal environment, including his body temperature; one thing is certain: none of us can instruct our body's systems to make the needed corrections beyond a very limited number of rather trivial tricks made possible by biofeedback techniques. If something goes wrong with my liver or my kidneys, I have no advice to offer out of my cortex, I rely on the system to fix itself, which it usually does with no help from me beyond crossing my fingers.

The running battle now in progress between the

sociobiologists and the antisociobiologists is a marvel for students to behold, close up. To observe, in open-mouthed astonishment, at the polarized extremes, one group of highly intelligent, beautifully trained, knowledgeable, and imaginative scientists maintaining that all sorts of behavior, animal and human, are governed exclusively by genes, and another group of equally talented scientists saying precisely the opposite and asserting that all behavior is set and determined by the environment, or by culture, and both sides brawling in the pages of periodicals like the *New York Review of Books*, is an educational experience that no college student should be allowed to miss. The essential lesson to be learned has nothing to do with the relative validity of the facts underlying the argument; it is the argument itself that is the education: we do not yet know enough to settle such questions.

One last example. There is an uncomfortable secret in biology, not much talked about yet, but beginning at last to surface. It is, in a way, linked to the observations which underlie the Gaia Hypothesis. Nature abounds in instances of cooperation and collaboration, partnerships between species. There is a tendency of living things to join up whenever joining is possible. Accommodation and compromise are more common in interliving than combat and destruction. Given the opportunity and the proper circumstances, two cells from totally different species—a mouse cell and a human cell, for example—will fuse together to become a single cell, and then the two nuclei will fuse into a single nucleus, and then the hybrid cell will divide to produce generations of new cells containing the combined genomes of both species. Bacteria are indispensable partners in the fixation of atmospheric nitrogen by plants. The oxygen in our atmosphere is put there, almost in its entirety, by the photosynthetic chloroplasts in the cells of green plants, and these organelles are almost certainly the descendants of blue-green algae which joined up when the nucleated cells of higher plants came into existence. The mitochondria in all our own cells, and in all other eukaryotic nucleated cells, which enable us to use oxygen for energy, are the direct descendants of symbiotic bacteria. These are becoming accepted facts, and there is no longer an agitated argument over their probable validity, but there are no satisfactory explanations for how such amiable and useful arrangements came into being in the first place. Axelrod and Hamilton[3] have recently reopened the question of cooperation in evolution, with a mathematical approach based on game theory (the Prisoner's Dilemma game) which permits the theory that one creature's best strategy for dealing with another, different creature is to concede and cooperate rather than defect and go it alone.

This idea can be made to fit with the mathematical justification based on kinship already proposed for explaining altruism in nature. It is, by the way, an interesting aspect of contemporary biology that true altruism, the giving away of something without return, is incompatible with dogma, even though it goes on all over the place. Nature, in this respect, keeps breaking the rules and needs correcting by new ways of doing arithmetic.

There isn't much of an argument yet about the human mind, which is, I suppose, the most formidable and complex of all the problems in nature which confront the human mind. Up until just recently we seem to have agreed all around that we have so little understanding of how our brains work that there's nothing much to talk about, much less fight over. But now the computer scientists have emerged with their huge, terrifying machines, imitating human calculation and thought, and there will soon be rancorous debates. The discussions are still low-key and polite, since nobody can argue intelligibly with a computer scientist except another computer scientist, and they are all too busy at their consoles to turn their heads. But the day will come, sooner or later, and I hope the college students will be trained in the jargon, familiar with the hardware, and sitting within close range of the raised voices.

I wrote a couple of essays a few years back on computers, in which I had a few things to say in opposition to the idea that machines could be made with what the computer people themselves call *Artificial Intelligence;* they always use capital letters for this technology, and refer to it in their technical papers as *AI.* I was not fond of the idea and said so, and proceeded to point out the necessity for error in the working of the human mind, which I thought made it different from the computer. In response, I received a great deal of mail, most of it gently remonstrative, but friendly (the worst kind of mail to get on days when things aren't going well anyway) pointing out to me in the simplest language how wrong indeed I was. Computers do proceed, of course, by the method of trial and error. The whole technology is based on this, can work in no other way.

One of the things I have always disliked about computers is that they are personally humiliating. They do resemble, despite my wish for it to be otherwise, the operations of the human mind. There are differences, but the Artificial Intelligence people, with their vast and clever computers, have come far enough along to make it clear that the machines behave like thinking machines. If they are right, the thing to worry about is not that they will ultimately be making electronic minds superior to ours, but that already ours are so inferior to theirs [mine anyway]. I have never heard of a computer, even a simple one, as dedicated to the deliberate process of forgetting information, losing it, restoring it out of context and in misleading forms, or generating such a condition of diffuse, inaccurate confusion, as occurs every day in the average human brain. We are already so outclassed as to live in constant embarrassment.

I have been inputting, as they say, one bit of hard data after another into my brain all my life, some of it thruputting and outputting from the other ear, but a great deal held and stored somewhere, or so I am assured, but I possess no reliable device, anywhere in my circuitry, for retrieving it when needed. If I wish for the simplest of things, someone's name for example, I cannot send in a straightforward demand with any sure hope of getting back the right name. I am often required to think about something else, something quite unrelated, and wait, hanging around in the mind's lobby, and then, if it is a lucky day, out pops the name. No computer could be designed by any engineer to function, or malfunction, in this way.

I have learned, one time or another, all sorts of things that I remember learning, but now they are lost to me. I cannot place the Thirty Years War or the Hundred Years War in the right centuries, nor have I at hand the barest facts about the issues involved. I once knew Keats. Lots of Keats by heart; he is still there, I suppose, probably scattered across the lobes of my left hemisphere, or maybe translated into the wordless language of my right hemisphere and preserved there forever as a set of hunches, but irretrievable as language. I have lost most of the philosophers I studied and liked long ago; the only sure memory I retain of Heidegger, even when I reread him today, is bewilderment. I have forgotten how to do cube roots, and will never learn again. Slide rules. Solid geometry. Thomas Hardy. Chinese etymology, which I tried to learn in great volumes just a few years ago. Where the numbers and letters are located on a dial telephone.

It occurs to me that the computer-brain analogy needs to take account of what must otherwise seem an unnatural degree of fallibility on the part of the brain. Maybe what we do, by compulsion, in order to make sure that our minds are always reasonably well prepared to get us through any new day, is something like what happens to a computer when you walk past it carrying a powerful magnet. Perhaps we are in possession of similar devices — maybe chemical messengers of some sort — that periodically sweep the mind clear of surplus information, leaving the chips and circuits open to the new needs of the day. I cannot remember Keats because he was erased one day; if I want him back, which I don't very badly, I am obliged to learn him all over again; he is gone out of the lobes where I had him once lodged.

In a way, this could be a reassuring notion, especially for anyone getting on in years. It would be nice to know that I have a mechanism, even if it is beyond my control, for editing away the accumulations of old and no longer usable information. Indeed, if there were not such a mechanism, the brain would sooner or later be stuffed, swollen, bulging with facts and unable to take in anything new. Signs would have to be displayed in all the lobes, reading *Occupied.* Or *No Entry.* Or, worst of all, signs repainted, changed to read *Exit.*

Come to think of it, you could not run a human brain in any other way, and the clearing out of excess information must be going on, automatically, all the time. Perhaps there are certain pieces of thought that must be classed as nonbiodegradable, like addition and one's family's names and how to read a taxi meter, but a great deal of material is surely disposable. Computers cannot do this sort of thing on their own. They can perform feats of mathematics beyond my comprehension, construct animated graphs at the touch of a finger, write with ease something like second-rate poetry, and they can even generate surprise for the operator, but I doubt very much that a computer, no matter how large and intricate, can itself make room for being surprised, *feel* surprised. There is not enough room for that in a computer the size of the galaxy.

Computers are good at seeing patterns, better than we are. They can connect up things that seem unrelated to each other, scanning the night sky or the stained blotches of 50,000 proteins on an electrophoretic gel or the numbers generated by all the world's stock markets, and find relationships that matter. We do something like this with our brains but we do it differently; we get things wrong. We use information not so much for its own sake as for leading to thoughts that really are unrelated, unconnected, and sometimes therefore quite new. If the human brain had not possessed this special gift we would still be sharpening bones, muttering to ourselves, unable to make a poem, or even whistle.

These two gifts, the ability to lose information unpredictably and to get relationships wrong, distinguish our brains from any computer I can imagine ever being manufactured. Artificial Intelligence is one thing, and I never spend a day without admiring it, but human intelligence is something else again.

This is not to say that I do not respect my brain, or anyone else's brain. I do, and I count it an added mark of respect to acknowledge that I do not understand it. My own mind, fallible, error-prone, forgetful, unpredictable, and ungovernable, is away over my head.

The social scientists are up to the hardest business of all, trying to understand how humanity works. They are caught up in debates all over town; everything they touch turns out to be one of society's nerve endings, eliciting outrage and cries of pain, and they are only at their beginning. Wait until they begin coming close to the bone, as they surely will someday, provided they can continue to attract enough bright people fascinated by humanity, unafraid of big numbers, and skeptical of question-naires, and provided the government does not starve them out of business as is now being tried in Washington. Politicians do not like pain, not even wincing, and they have some fear of what the social scientists may be thinking about thinking for the future.

The social scientists are themselves too modest about the history of their endeavor, tending to display only the matters under scrutiny today in economics, sociology, and psychology; for example, never boasting, as they might, about one of the greatest of all scientific advances in our comprehension of humanity, for which they could be claiming credit. I refer here, of course, to the marvelous accomplishments of the nineteenth century comparative linguists. When the scientific method is working at its best, it succeeds in revealing the connection between things in nature that seem at first totally unrelated to each other. Long before the time when the biologists, led by Darwin and Wallace, were constructing the tree of evolution and the origin of species, the linguists were hard at work on the evolution of language. Beginning with Sir William Jones in 1786 and his inspired hunch that the remarkable similarities between Sanskrit, Greek, and Latin meant, in his words, that these three languages must "have sprung from some common source, which, perhaps, no longer exists," the new science of comparative grammar took off in 1816 with Franx Bopp's classic work entitled "On the conjugational system of the Sanskrit language in comparison with that of the Greek, Latin, Persian, and Germanic languages," a piece of work equivalent, in its scope and in its power to explain, to the best of the nineteenth century biology. The common Indoeuropean ancestry of English, Germanic, Slavic, Greek, Latin, Baltic, Indic, Iranian, Hittite, and Anatolian tongues, and the meticulous scholarship worked out in detail for connecting these languages, was a tour de force for research, science at its best, and social science at that. Modern linguistics has moved into new areas of inquiry as specialized and inaccessible for most laymen (including me) as particle physics; I cannot guess at where it will come out, but it is surely aimed at scientific comprehension and its problem, human language, is as crucial for the species as any other field I can think of, including molecular genetics.

But there are some risks involved in trying to do science in the humanities before its time, and useful lessons can be learned from some of the not-so-distant history of medicine. A century ago it was the common practice to deal with disease by analyzing what then seemed to be the underlying mechanism, and by applying whatever treatment popped into the doctor's head. Congestion of the body fluids and the backing up of blood in various organs, an imaginary concept dating back to Galen in the first century, was still regarded as the underlying process to be corrected, and patients with tuberculosis or typhoid fever were bled within an inch of their lives, purged into shock, sometimes poisoned by massive doses of mercury, bismuth, and arsenic. Getting sick was a hazardous enterprise in those days. The driving force in medicine was to *do* something, never mind what. It occurs to me now, reading in incomprehension some of the current reductionist writings in literary criticism, especially poetry criticism, that the new schools are at risk under a similar pressure. A poem is assumed to be a kind of illness, needing treatment; bleed it white, purge it, blister it, draw out the meaning along with all the meanings, deconstruct it, *do* something, never mind what. This could be a biological mistake. A poem is a healthy organism, really, in need of no help from science, no treatment except fresh air and exercise. I thought I'd just sneak that in.

NOTES

1. Lovelock, James E. *Gaia: A New Look at Life on Earth* (New York, Oxford University Press, 1978).

2. Doolittle, W. Ford. "Is Nature Really Motherly?" *Co-Evolution Quarterly* 29 (Spring 1981) pp. 62-63. In the same issue are responses by Lovelock, pp. 62-63, and by Margulis, pp. 63-65.

3. Axelrod, Robert, and Hamilton, Wm. D. "The Evolution of Cooperation," *Science* 211, 1981, pp. 1390-1396.

The High School-College Connection

Connection

BY FRED HECHINGER

CHAPTER SIX

*T*wo years or so ago, I was watching "Roots II" with our younger son, who was then about twelve. In that particular segment we saw a young, black noncommissioned marine officer who had just come back from World War II. He and his young wife and their baby were driving away from the battleship on which he had served. They were on their way home somewhere in the South, and as evening fell, they stopped at a motel to seek lodging for the night. There was a big vacancy sign outside the motel, but when the young marine went in to get a room he was told there wasn't any. They stopped at another motel, and another, and a fourth, and a fifth. Each time it was the same story until it became finally clear that this young man, still in his uniform, and his wife and the baby would have to sleep in the car along the road.

At that point, John, our son, turned to me and said, "Daddy, that couldn't really have happened, could it?" Suddenly it dawned on me that what was absolutely part of my history, of knowing what had been happening in the country in my experience, was not part of his. And when the young men and women in our schools and colleges talk about World

War II, they are most likely to conjure up very little else but the one thing that the revisionist historians have told them over and over again — the crime of bombing Dresden and Hiroshima. This is the big story in the experience or nonexperience of many of these young people who obviously have no connection with World War II, and who therefore judge everything they hear about that war only in the terms of Hai Phong. Vietnam, after all, is the only war they know and the new high school and college generation does not even remember Vietnam or the civil rights marches, let alone Pearl Harbor.

The point is that when we talk about general education we cannot assume that the young will automatically make the connection with events and ideas that were part of our own lives but not theirs. Yet, there is an urgent need to help them make that connection. We need to connect with what came before us and is not part of our experience, and to make a connection, not only with the past but, we hope, with the future too.

American education has become a collection of disjointed parts that fail to connect. It is in many ways like a play with a succession of scenes and acts, each written by a different playwright and staged by a different director. Good things happen in some segments, but they do not add up to a satisfying whole. The central character, the student, ends up without any sense of unity. In the mid-sixties, for example, we created Project Headstart to help underprivileged children escape from their mind-eroding environment. In the years that followed, the greatest threat to that very successful new program turned out to be the inability of the elementary school, and subsequently the secondary school, to build on what already had been accomplished.

That example was symptomatic of a succession of vertical divisions in our educational enterprise. There is little continuity of plan or purpose between elementary and junior high schools and between high schools and colleges. In the 1960s, critics of the American schools' view of the world said that what was wrong with how history was taught was that it assumed that the world began in Athens and ended in California. Those who objected to a study of civilization based on the ideas of Western superiority, the civilization closest to us, had, of course, a point. But a much more fundamental flaw than mere parochialism was overlooked in this criticism. That flaw was the defective study of even that limited slice of the Euro-American Western heritage.

That deficiency has not been corrected by the subsequent addition of the study of some non-Western cultures. It has merely crowded a few new dishes into an unsatisfactory smorgasbord. Not long ago, when Stanford University was debating the reintroduction of a general education requirement of Western civilization, I talked to some of the students. One student leader, otherwise a very bright young man, said he objected to Western civilization because it was racist. I asked him to look at some other civilizations and tell me how racist or nonracist they were, and whether that really made any difference to the requirement to study them.

*T*wo fundamental questions need to be asked in any attempt to make connections, and they are questions our schools and colleges really are not asking themselves in spite of the fact that they are talking about the broad issues. Those questions are: Who is responsible for teaching the basic skills? Who takes care of general education? How do the two connect? The first is preparation and the second is the central core of the whole process of education. Both are, as we know, in disarray. They suffer from the lack of continuity that plagues American education in general.

Instead of connecting the separate levels, critics compound the spirit of separation by encouraging the typical reaction of the American society to existing deficiencies: to seek scapegoats, instead of remedies, for what has gone wrong. Professionals at each level point accusing fingers at the level below. And, in the case of the grade schools, where there is no professional level below, they point the finger at the parents. It is always somebody else's fault that the requirements have not been fulfilled. In one of the oldest games of American pedagogy, university academicians rail against the weaknesses of teacher-training institutions and of high school teachers, without taking an active hand in helping to correct what are, in fact, serious deficiencies.

Good elementary school teachers could do a great deal to teach high school teachers and even college teachers how to deal with people. I had a teacher in third grade who encouraged me to write poems, and then he surprised me on my birthday: he had set one of my poems to music, and not only that, he presented it to me in a beautiful folder, which he had illustrated with lovely pen sketches. He had done more for the cause of general education, the respect for words, the introduction of music, the embellishment of art, than any lecture could have done, and I must say that, since then, few of my teachers have lived up to that example. That is precisely what

I mean when I say that many elementary school teachers could help us even with the effort to turn graduate teaching assistants into real teachers.

Recently, a national survey indicated a decline in high school students' mathematical performance. I wanted to write a story about it, and went down a list of noted university mathematicians, calling them up to ask what they thought might be wrong in the teaching of high school mathematics. With one exception, they were puzzled by my question, and they replied by asking: "How would we know? We don't know what's happening in high schools." They did know that something was wrong in the high schools, but they could not define it; they did not know what was happening and why; and they were not helping the teachers.

Excessive stress on remediation compounds the lack of continuity. When remediation experts are expected by the education establishment to pick up the pieces years later, as in remedial reading instruction in high school or college, the process of orderly progression turns into disarray. There is not sufficient expectation that the remedial job will be accomplished at the proper level.

Thus I am not as sanguine as some about the future of general education. I join Ernie Boyer in finding the neglect of general education very disconcerting. While we have no real definition of it, we all agree that it is part of the basic baggage educated men and women should be expected to carry when they leave school. It is the foundation of knowledge and understanding on which people should be able to build for the rest of their lives. It underlies their comprehension of politics and economics; their capacity to stretch their minds through books, as consumers of the arts, as independent thinkers, as guides for their children.

$\mathcal{T}$oday's concern with continuing education and lifelong learning loses much of its meaning and promise if adult learners come to it without that foundation of general education on which to build. I do not share the view of those who think the modern world is too complex to be dealt with in an approach to general education. If college faculties tell me, as they've told some of you, that it can't be done, then I consider them deficient teachers.

I am reminded of an experiment in general education at Amherst College in the late forties. It was significant because Amherst was not a very progressive institution and yet it managed to launch a college-wide experiment that survived a number of years and inspired other colleges. The capstone, the centerpiece, of this program was a course taken by all students in the sophomore year called "Problems in American Democracy." The twelve or thirteen problems discussed each year were picked by the faculty, who also wrote the textbooks containing the original papers and source materials. The resulting series of paperbacks, incidentally, were subsequently published commercially and widely used. But the important aspect of the course was not any particular problems, but the fact that the effort involved the entire student body and the entire faculty, without question of discipline or rank. The arts, the humanities, the sciences, all participated, along with outside consultants, speakers, and lecturers, ranging from the Secretary of State to visiting academicians, and even an occasional newspaperman. All of them worked together in testifying that the world was not too complex to be looked at, discussed rationally, and studied sensibly by the entire academic community. I suspect that while this program did not solve the problem of teaching students final answers, it accomplished what was described at the Colloquium on Common Learning as giving students at least an informed bewilderment, and that's a great deal to accomplish.

At the time, I asked one of the founders of this particular program to describe its goals. He said, "All we expect is to teach the students to consider the consequences of their actions." I think that is a definition of goals that could go a long way toward building some sound general education programs.

*T*he question, then, is: Who takes care of the vital building blocks in this enterprise?

In the European model, from which American education borrowed so heavily, general education is largely the concern of the secondary school, the lycée, the gymnasium, the grammar school. It is there that a carefully mapped-out curriculum teaches history, geography, literature, mathematics, science, as well as foreign languages. (Incidentally, at a recent international meeting, European representatives were absolutely stunned to learn that it is possible to graduate from an American college or university without ever having studied a foreign language.) In the European model, all of these elements of general education are studied in natural progression by all students. A British graduate of a secondary school who enters the university is expected to be liberally educated and a candidate for specialized higher education. The American experience has been quite different, and the difference represents a substantial advance toward a more open and egalitarian school system and, with it, society. Instead of presorting children early, usually at age ten or eleven, the American school made a firm commitment to educate all children through the high school. This is a tall order because it requires incomparably broader skills to teach so wide a range of capacities. Under ideal circumstances, in exceptional schools, the American approach has outdistanced anything that has ever been tried anywhere.

More often, American schools have surrendered to the much easier way — lowering their sights to the comfortable common denominator. In most schools, the prescribed curriculum has long since given way to a cafeteria-style education menu, with general education requirements reduced to the bare minimum. Periodically, efforts were made to reverse this trend. In 1959, for instance, James Conant responded to the erosion by creating, for a brief period, a high school curriculum that aimed at a revival of general education.

But whatever momentary progress was made at that time was erased by the revolt against all requirements in the sixties. Many school administrators caved in as the political and pedagogical camp followers of the great youth movement extolled the virtues of an education freed of all traditional constraints. Instant relevancy took precedence over any systematic study of the past. Revisionist historians and educators scoffed at courses rooted in Western civilization as sterile, if not counterrevolutionary.

Under such conditions, continuity in American education, which had never been strongly established in the first place, suffered a severe setback. Students entered college with only the most sketchy general knowledge, and, compounding the damage, general education in the colleges also was seriously weakened in the same period. General education requirements gave way to an open-ended system of "anything goes."

In the absence of any effective contact between school and college faculties, no deliberate effort was made to fill the void, perhaps because nobody cared to determine the extent of that void. And, since the students themselves had become preoccupied with preprofessional or precareer concerns, they shunned the general education courses in college just as they had done in high school. At the collegiate level, I should add, remedial instruction in the basic skills of reading, writing, and mathematics, which the disjointed system had failed to teach earlier, took away even more of the time that might have been given to general education.

Perhaps the ultimate proof of this flawed nature of a system of discontinuity is the growing demand for an infusion of humanities courses in graduate and professional schools to fill the void left at the lower levels. As you know, this is a strong movement at present in law schools and, particularly, in medical schools. (Anyone who has recently spent time in a hospital knows that this infusion of the humanities does not come any too soon.) In theory, there is nothing inherently wrong with the addition of a new dimension to education at that high level; but in practice, it is probably too much to expect the average student facing the intense pressures of graduate and professional studies to be very receptive to these efforts to catch up with what should have been taught in school and college. Such a remedial approach is, at the very least, inefficient, whether it deals with basic writing or a fundamental knowledge of the humanities and the sciences.

We hear much today about the need for quality controls, and this brings to mind a recent report by a correspondent who had returned from Japan where he interviewed the managing director of an electronics manufacturing company. He

had asked the Japanese manager to define the difference between quality control in American and Japanese industry, and
the Japanese, trying to be as polite as he could, said "You, in
the United States, try to control quality by detection, and we
try to control it by prevention." Less politely put, this means
"we try to make it work the first time," and, you might add,
teaching children to read in first and second grade. Lack of
continuity means postponement, leaving to tomorrow what
should have been tackled yesterday. In education, tomorrow
too regularly never comes.

This puts education out of synchronization with human
developments. To use the most drastic example, missing the
opportunity of teaching a foreign language to children at age
seven or eight or even younger, places an unnecessary and
unproductive mental burden on the teenagers or undergraduates or graduate students who, for the first time, try to
cope with what would have been hardly any effort at all if it
had been begun at the proper level of education. Equally
wasteful is the teaching of foreign languages in elementary
school, dropping it from the curriculum in junior high or high
school, and then, five or six years later, at the time of the
graduate dissertation, suddenly requiring and expecting that
a student pick up the language that he or she dropped so long
ago.

*T*he fact that the discontinuity may not always
be so obvious in other subjects makes it no less subversive of
sound education. The demand for ethics courses in law school
merely underscores the lack of coordination between law

school deans, school superintendents, and college departmental chairmen. Following the recent introduction of a new and more mature college textbook in American history, it was reported that one teacher received this complaint from his students: "It's nice to read about the rise of Jacksonian democracy, but just who the hell is Andrew Jackson?"

The need is to establish a continuity in education that involves scholars and teachers at all levels in planning the entire enterprise. The goal is not to eliminate repetition of what is being taught in grade school, junior high school, high school, college, and thereafter. It is rather to differentiate, to cite an example, between the depth and sophistication that may be appropriate, say, to a ten-year-old who is introduced to the question of ethical behavior, and what may be appropriate for a college freshman dealing with the same issues. In history, the same period may be studied in high school, concentrating on facts and events or on cause and effect, and in college, with emphasis on concepts and ideas. Students so prepared would not be tempted to ask that question about Andrew Jackson.

School-college curriculum planners should ensure that no gaping holes are left in the students' progress toward some educational and human maturity. Perhaps the foundation for any real continuity ought to begin with an understanding that there cannot be any educational or human enterprise without respect for language.

I was horrified not long ago, in a report on an international conference on hunger in the world, to see the starving countries identified over and over again as "nutritionally unstable." It is of a piece with a government directive that was sent out a few years ago telling federal agencies not to use the term *poverty* in their papers, and to replace it with *low-*

income. It was a great accomplishment: overnight we had wiped out poverty. Unfortunately, the poor know the difference between low-income and poverty. I cite this only as example of the importance of language, respect for language, and proper use of language as the foundation for any effort to give young people that shared baggage of general education.

Fortunately, efforts to cope with the problem of discontinuity need not begin from scratch. The introduction of advanced placement courses many years ago was aimed at precisely that kind of problem. But it was a selective, and not a total approach. It had some of the makings of a customs union between school and college, and that was good. But a more deliberate strategy is needed, reaching out to affect the education of all students, not just the relatively few outstanding college-preparatory high school students.

Science occasionally has provided us with useful models, perhaps because scientists today tend to take a broader view of the world and of education than many of their colleagues in the humanities and social sciences. Seeing the effect of what is taught to children in elementary school on their future development as scientifically illiterate adolescents and adults alarms scientists. Scientists are also more prone to view their students as junior partners. Led by scientists, a hardy band of university professors in the 1950s made a stab at continuity. Jerrold Zacharias, Bentley Glass, and a number of others worked with high school teachers to improve the teaching of science and, at the same time, to improve the state of general education. Much of the progress of those days has since been dissipated. School and college educators have again gone their separate ways, though there are signs of some new interest in getting together. Educational technology, which promises to make an unprecedented impact on schools is a natural catalyst for school/university cooperation. Such pioneers as Seymour Papert at MIT, with his combination of technological-mathematical training and his practical experience in child development through years of partnership with Piaget could be enlisted in the search for continuing learning of this kind. Harvard's Graduate School of Education has recently turned its attention to the study and support of elementary and high school principals in their day-to-day work with children. In Chicago, Benjamin Bloom, the child psychologist, is providing models for a new strategy of mass relearning in the early grades as a means of putting an end to the postponement of the children's acquisition of the tools for study. At the University of California, Los Angeles, John Goodlad is carrying out similar experiments.

*I*f a beginning has been made in the essential task of creating a new continuity in American education, the nationwide search for some effective central or core curriculum in the undergraduate years is a welcome change. But to be fully effective, these curricular changes ought to be worked out jointly by school and college faculties and administrators—not to divide the field, but to join the two cultures at all levels of teaching and learning. It may not be a politically easy move to make, but a determined policy of creating continuity calls for plans to phase out much of the remedial work now being carried on in high school and college. Already, too many of the special faculty departments engaged in such catch-up teaching constitute a vested interest group that is hard to reduce in numbers and funding. But their very presence eases the pressure on the elementary and junior high schools to do the job of teaching the basic skills. An orderly retreat from such responsibility by the colleges, without inhumane shortchanging of those underprepared students already in the pipeline, is essential to the establishment of an effective progression from elementary school through high school through college.

American education rightly takes pride in the fact that it has been open-ended and flexible. One way of beginning the search for ways leading to effective general education might be to include in the study of American history at all levels the importance of education to American society. This is one of the largely ignored chapters in most American historians' accounts of the 200 years of the American story.

American education is more than the school. It is the foundation of our society. If we want to learn more about the general sharing of knowledge and the responsibility of school and college, students must learn about the unique responsibility education has taken on and must continue to assume, for the perpetuation of an open society. We have only begun the essential task of connecting the links of a chain that is now badly damaged and torn to create a common learning in which all who teach will share the responsibility and, ultimately, the joy.

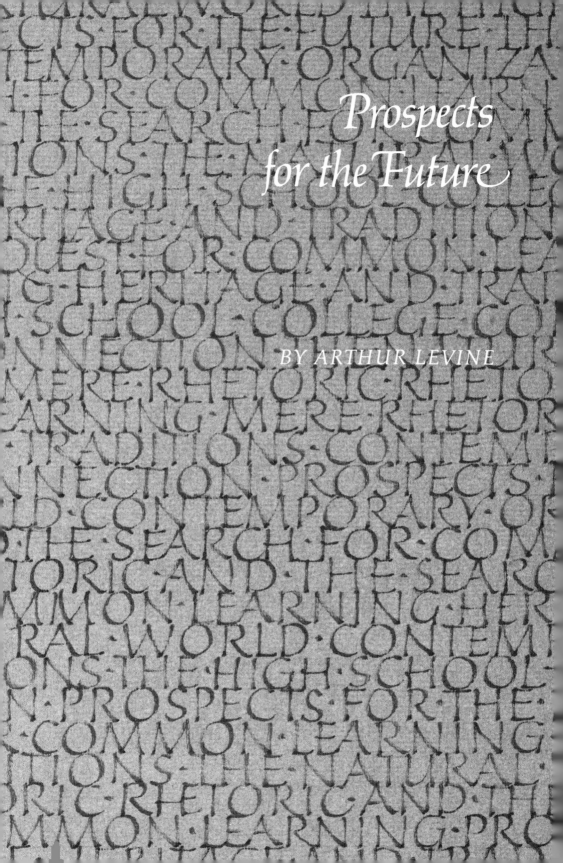

Prospects
for the Future

BY ARTHUR LEVINE

CHAPTER SEVEN

*F*our years ago, the Carnegie Foundation for the Advancement in Teaching described general education as a "disaster area." What can be said about its health today? What can we expect for tomorrow?

There is good news and there is bad news. The bad news is that I have been looking at general education programs around the country, and, by and large, they are not working.

Many are lacking in coherence and purpose.

There is a tendency for programs to be more specialized than general. Too often, they are geared to the needs of departments instead of the needs of common learning.

Requirements at many institutions are satisfied by instruction that seems to be randomly chosen from a grab bag of unrelated courses.

Students tend to rate the quality of current general education classes below average.

Rewards and incentives for faculty participation in general education are meager and, in a number of cases, negative.

This is pretty sobering stuff!

But it brings us to the good news, which is simply this—
the prospects for improving general education are better today
than they have been in years.

One need not be a Pollyanna to see this. Anyone who has
attended a university knows that the barriers to general education are great. Curriculum reform is never easy. Few faculty are
willing to devote themselves to general education, and student
enrollment in general education classes has declined in recent
years.

Yet, without being unduly optimistic, it is important to
realize that the mood of America's colleges and universities is
changing. There is a very real desire to reform general education
today.

In 1978, an ad was placed in the *Chronicle of Higher Education* asking
for volunteer institutions to work on a project aimed at changing their
general education programs. There were more than 300 expressions of
interest. That represents one out of every ten colleges in the country.

This interest has been matched by action. In comparison with five
years ago, general education requirements for the baccalaureate have
increased substantially. Despite declines in mathematics and foreign
languages, nearly one third more colleges and universities have science requirements. A quarter more require social science. A fifth
more require English composition. Up, too, are humanities, fine arts,
and religion.

It seems like every school Ernest Boyer and I visit lately is rethinking
or revising its general education program. Last year alone, the Foundation was in contact with more than 200 schools, and that is a
conservative estimate.

The prospects for improving general education today are
excellent for three reasons.

First, the timing is right. General education is consistent with the current mood of the campus and the nation. It is perceived to be a remedy for the crises that currently confront us. In fact, it is touted as the answer to almost every educational and social problem we face.

It is being called upon to respond to the trauma of Watergate by providing moral training to young people and resetting the ethical compass of the nation.

It is being asked to combat the isolationism that swept the country in the aftermath of the Vietnam war and to provide a global perspective at a time when it is painfully obvious that the fate of this nation is determined by events beyond its border.

It is seen as an antidote to "the new narcissism," a way to jolt the "me generation" from its myopic self-obsession.

It is viewed as a means of introducing a fragmented and divided nation with declining interest in civic responsibility and increasing pessimism about the future to a common heritage and to problems we all face together.

It is embraced as the answer to declining student academic performance, as a way of combatting the curricular movement from the 3 Rs (reading, writing, and arithmetic) to the 6 Rs (remedial reading, remedial writing, and remedial arithmetic).

It is also thought of as a palliative for the "New Vocationalism," the increasing career orientation and declining interest of today's undergraduates in the liberal arts.

It is sought as a remedy for academic overspecialization, the rising concentration in major studies that resulted from the elimination of general requirements in the 1960s.

Second, there is evidence that students are much more per-ceptive to general education than is generally supposed.

A study by the Carnegie Council on Policy Studies in Higher Education revealed that 97 percent of a representative sample of college students considered general education an "essential" or "fairly important" part of their college education.

This year's college freshmen ranked general education as one of the top three reasons for seeking higher education at all.

Here's the catch. Undergraduates also report that they are enormously dissatisfied with the general education programs their colleges offer. In a recent study of ten institutions representative of the diversity of higher education (four liberal arts colleges, four universities, a community college, and one technical institution) Jerry Gaff found that although 94 percent of the students wanted general education, only 20 percent were very satisfied with the courses they had taken. By way of comparison, at least twice as many students reported satisfaction with their academic majors and electives.

The nation's colleges and universities have misinterpreted student dissatisfaction with their general education *courses* as a distaste for general education. In the hope of mitigating the problem, colleges have watered down the content of their classes and sugar-coated their courses. In so doing, they have only exacerbated the problem.

There is every reason to believe that today's students will support general education if a well-shaped program is constructed. This is true not only because students express interest in general education, but also because they express interest in jobs. This generation is more concerned about careers, money, and material goods than their predecessors of a decade ago were, and this, ironically, will make general education more appealing to them.

Strict vocational training is excellent for preparing students for a first job. It is far better at this than is general education alone. But vocational training by itself often fails to provide students with the skills to leave that first job. At building the succession of jobs we call a career, it does poorly. A combination of vocational and general education is needed to make the difference between a job and a career.

Study after study of alumni, professionals, and executives has consistently produced the same findings. Individuals out of college up to three years describe their undergraduate education as deficient in providing instruction. Seven years following school and thereafter, however, they indicate that their careers would have been significantly enhanced if they had had more general education.

From this perspective, general education not only makes educational sense, it makes dollars and cents. And this is a perspective that will be particularly attractive to current college students.

Third, faculty members are more supportive of general education now than in the recent past. A plurality, some 47 percent, favor a common core of studies for all of the students at their institution. In contrast, only 6 percent believe a free-elective curriculum would be preferable.

Faculty participation in general education is on the rise at many institutions. Declining enrollments and financial need are making it more attractive. A good example is a well-known eastern research university. In the 1960s, virtually no senior faculty member chose to participate in general education; junior staffers and the least able graduate students were unwillingly assigned to teach the courses in the program. Staff turnover was about 50 percent each year; morale was low; and the quality of the general education course was continually poor. Students rated the courses far below the university average. At one point, the history department even withdrew support from the program and refused to supply it with faculty.

This has changed. Faculty in liberal arts departments at this university now face declining enrollments. Even the best graduate students cannot get financial help. So underenrolled departments, undersubscribed faculty, and underfinanced graduate students are begging to teach Western Civilization. In fact, the chairman of the history department, which has lost enrollment in recent years, is now director of the program.

To be sure, this is only one institution. But this same shift in priorities is occurring at other schools too.

In the current era of retrenchment, when several institutions are cutting back a proliferating number of departmental courses and replacing them with a smaller number of higher enrollment general education classes, common learning is gaining a certain positive appeal. More adversity made the difference. For one thing, faculty members grow tired of teaching the same courses year after year. Also, in a leaner curriculum, general education is one place where creative planning can still take place. As one professor put it, general education is the only home for experimentation remaining on campus. It is not unusual today for faculty members to actually choose teaching in general education for its excitement and stimulation.

$\mathcal{G}$eneral education reform has a great deal going for it today—timing, student interest, and enhanced faculty support.

All of this is necessary, but I do not mean to imply that it is sufficient. Determined colleges and universities will have to do more if improvement is to occur. At a minimum, they will have to:

Make their commitment to general education explicit

Reallocate resources to support general education

Provide rewards and incentives to faculty and departments that participate in general education

Remove the traditional stigma from general education instruction by encouraging the best faculty members — senior as well as junior people—to teach in general education

Provide opportunities for faculty and staff to improve both their skills and their understanding of general education

Grant released time for faculty to develop new general education courses

Evaluate general education courses early and often in nonthreatening ways.

Nonetheless, I remain quite optimistic about the prospects for general education. Sociologists tell us that change is most likely to occur under five conditions:

1. *When the environment is in crisis*—For example, when colleges have found their enrollments declining, the rate of change has accelerated. This occurred in the 1840s and 1850s, when colleges fell into public disfavor; during the major wars

of this century, when the students were drafted; and during the current era of demographic shifts.

2. *When change is consistent with self-interest* — That is, if people are worried about their jobs and the possible closure of their colleges, as is the case today at many institutions, change is more likely to occur. It was precisely under these circumstances that a struggling liberal arts college named St. John's adopted a Great Books program in 1937.

3. *When there is a power imbalance in the environment* — This is the situation with the panoply of changes that occurred during the 1960s in the wake of student unrest.

4. *When there is structural change in the environment* — For example, it was the building of a new dormitory that encouraged Bowdoin College to rethink its undergraduate program and to create a senior center and a senior year general education program.

5. *When change is consistent with the* zeitgeist *or spirit of the times.*

Three of these conditions support general education reform today:

There is a sense of crisis in our country and on our campuses, and general education is perceived to be a remedy for many of the problems — for the Watergate mentality, global isolationism, the new narcissism, declining student ability at basic skills, over vocationalism, and the rest.

General education is consistent with self-interest. It is a way to reduce the costs of instruction for financially troubled colleges. It is a means of providing students to needy departments, faculty, and graduate students.

Finally, general education reform is consistent with the spirit of the times. There is a general education revival going on in this country.

Historically, each of the five conditions by itself has been sufficient for curriculum change. The simultaneous existence of three of them is extraordinary, and makes the present a uniquely propitious time for strengthening general education. Quite frankly, I do not know that we will ever have a better opportunity.

The Authors

WAYNE C. BOOTH
Distinguished Service Professor and
former Dean of the College, University
of Chicago

ERNEST L. BOYER
President, The Carnegie Foundation
for the Advancement of Teaching

FRED M. HECHINGER
President, The New York Times
Company Foundation

ROSABETH MOSS KANTER
Professor of Sociology
Yale University

ARTHUR LEVINE
Senior Fellow, The Carnegie Foundation
for the Advancement of Teaching

FREDERICK RUDOLPH
Mark Hopkins Professor of History
Williams College

LEWIS THOMAS, M.D.
Chancellor, Memorial Sloan-
Kettering Cancer Research Center

INDEX

Acton, Lord, 70
Adams, Henry, 61, 70
Allen, Frederick Lewis, 4
Altruism in nature, 105-06
Amherst College, 4, 120
Animal awareness, 101-03
Aristotle, 31
Arnold, Thomas, 54
Axelrod, Robert, 106

Beliefs. *See* Shared values
Bloom, Benjamin, 127
Bopp, Franx, 111
Bowdoin College, 138
Brain: animal awareness, 101-03; human mind and computers compared, 106-10
Burke, Edmund, 15

Carr, E. H., 67-68
Carter, Jimmy, 29, 30
Chance, and evolution, 103-05
Change: conditions favorable to, 137-38; curriculum adaptation to, 60-61; institutional behavior and, 89-90
Chronicle of Higher Education, The, 43
Citizenship: general education and, 39; rhetoric and, 42-44; science and, 14-15
Clouser, K. Danner, 14
Coherency: and history, 15-16, 67-69; and science, 96
Columbia University, 4, 70-71
Common learning. *See* General education
Common life: general education focus on, 7-11; shared elements of, 11-17
Communication skills, 11-12, 125-26
Comparative linguistics, 111-12
Computers: computer language skills, 12; human mind compared, 106-10
Conant, James, 122
Continuing education, 120

Dartmouth College, 4
Denison University, 6
de Tocqueville, Alexis, 65
Donne, John, 64
Doolittle, W. Ford, 104
Double Helix, The (Watson), 45

Economics, and rhetoric, 46-47
Education system. *See* General
 education
Eliot, T. S., 15
Emerson, Ralph Waldo, 64
Equalitarianism: and disregard of
 history, 66, 67; and education
 system, 121-22
European education system, 121
Evolution, 99: chance and, 103-05;
 cooperation in, 105-06

Faculty: and discontinuity of education system, 118-19; inadequate rewards for, 18-19, 131;
 support for general education,
 135-36
Federalist Papers, The, 43
Ford, Henry, 57
Foreign language skill, 12, 124
Friedman, Milton, 47, 78

Gaff, Jerry, 134
Gaia Hypothesis, 104
Geertz, Clifford, 19
General education: Amherst experiment, 120-21; curriculum continuity requirement, 17-18,
 124-28; discontinuity between
 high school and college curricula,
 115-19; European experience,
 121; and focus on common life,
 7-11; kinds of generality, 37-40;
 neglect of, 3, 121-23, 131-32;
 previous reforms, 4-7; proposed
 themes for, 11-17; remedial instruction, 119, 123-24; renewed
 interest in, 19-20, 132-39
Glass, Bentley, 126
Goodlad, 127
Goodness: as goal of "whole man,"
 60; *See also* Truth
Goulden, Josephy C., 5
Griffin, Donald, 101-02

Hamilton, W. D., 106
Harvard University, 6, 70-72, 127
Haverford College, 23
High school curriculum. *See* General education
History: disregard for relevancy of, 57-59, 63-67, 122; incorporation into curriculum, 70-73; justification for study of, 15-16, 67-69; unconnected experience of, 115-17; "whole man" concept, 59-63
Humanities, remedial course, 123
Human mind. *See* Brain
Hutchins, Robert, 4

Identity: institutional influences on, 81-83; sense of, history and, 69; tentative sense of, 10, 65, 67; "whole man" awareness of, 62
Immigration, 65
Individualism: and disregard for history, 65-66; institutional limits on, 81-83; voluntaristic model of institutional behavior, 77-80

Institutions: emphasis on specialization, 75-77; and individual behavior, 81-83, 88-89; justification for study of, 12-13; management of, 91-92; recalcitrant behavior of, 83-91; voluntaristic behavior model, 77-80
Intelligence. *See* Brain

Japan, 88, 123-24
Jones, Sir William, 111

Kline, Morris, 40

Language: comparative linguistics, 111-12; foreign language skill, 12, 124; skill requirement, 11-12, 125-26
Lincoln, Abraham, 69
Locke, John, 7
Lovelock, James E., 104
Lucy (Johanson and Edey), 45

McKeon, Richard 38
Madison, James, 43
Mass communication: and individual's sense of time, 63-64; justification for study of, 12
Mathematics: and altruism, 106; and general field theory, 40; justification for study of, 11
Meiklejohn, Alexander, 4
Mind. *See* Brain

Natural world. *See* Science
Nonverbal communication, 12
Notes (Madison), 43
Numbers, usage skills, 11

Order, and science, 95-96
Organizations. *See* Institutions

Paine, Tom, 44
Papert, Seymour, 127
Polanyi, Michael, 45
Political skills. *See* Citizenship
Popper, Karl R., 48
Potts, David B., 71, 72
Premedical science, 97-99

Reagan, Ronald, 29-30
Reed College, 4
Remedial education, 119, 123-24
Rhetoric: as art of inquiry, 34-37; and citizenship, 42-44; and cross-cultural understanding, 48-49; as foundation for general education, 23-27, 40-42, 53-54; and history curriculum, 71; levels of, analysis, 27-34; and science, 44-48; and search for truth, 49-53
Rhetoric (Aristotle), 31, 54
Roosevelt, Franklin D., 68
Rosovsky, Henry, 71
Russell, Bertrand, 17

St. John's College, 138
School curriculum. *See* General education
Science: contemporary disputes in, 101-06; continuity between high school and college curricula, 126-27; and desire for order, 95-96; human mind and computers compared, 106-10; justification for study of, 14-15; mistakes in teaching of, 96-99; rhetoric and, 44-48; and understanding of humanity, 110-12; value of ambiguity in, 99-101
Scientific American, 47
Shared values: general education and, 39-40; justification for study of, 7, 16-17; rhetoric and, 48-49; value indoctrination curricula, 70-71
Sloan, Douglas, 72
Snow, C. P., 14
Snyder, Ned, 23
Social conditions; and change, 137-38; and education reform, 4-7, 133, 138-39
Social science, 110-12

Specialization: and bureaucratic rigidity, 85; institutional emphasis on, 75-77; as rejection of general education, 6, 9-10; "whole man" opposition to, 59-60
Stanford University, 117
Stone, Christopher, 86-87
Students: aversion to science, 97-99; support of general education, 134-35; vocational interests, 9-10, 123
Surprise: computer's inability to experience, 110; and science, 95, 99-100

Teachers. *See* Faculty
Television. *See* Mass communication
Thomas, Lewis, 10, 46
Truth: general education and, 40; search for, rhetoric and, 49-53

Union College, 71
University of California, 127
University of Chicago, 4, 42, 71, 127

Values. *See* Shared values
Van Doren, Mark, 9, 20
Veblen, Thorstein, 85
Vocational interests, 9-10, 123, 134-35

Weber, Max, 84
Wesleyan University, 6
Wilson, Woodrow, 9
Work, study of, 13

Zacharias, Jerrold, 126

Date Due